THE
WARDLE
STORY

Sir Thomas and Lady Wardle
A Victorian Enterprise

by

Anne Jacques
M.B.E.

Wardle.

CHURNET VALLEY BOOKS

Published by

CHURNET VALLEY BOOKS

43 Bath Street
Leek
Staffordshire
01538 399033

© Anne Jacques and Churnet Valley Books
1996

ISBN 1897949 17 0

Printed in Great Britain by The Ipswich Book Company, Suffolk

CONTENTS

PEDIGREE OF THE WARDLES OF LEEK

Joseph WARDLE
b. 1777
bur.1832

Martha EARLS
b. 1773
bur.1864
Leek
Cemetery

Mar.

Thomasina LEEKE
Heath Hse
Cheddleton

Hugh WARDLE
b. 1802
d. 1860

Joshua
bap.4.11.1802
Leek
bur. 1879
Cheddleton

Mary DARLINGTON
b. 1804
d. 1875

Mar.

George Young
d. 1910

Madeleine HAMILTON SMITH
d. 1928

Mar. 1861

Elizabeth
d. 1835
d. 1902

Thomas
b. 1831
d. 1909

Mar.

Elizabeth
b. 1833
d. 1912

John ILLSEY
b. 1862
d.1890

Mar.

George
b. 1836
d. 1912

Frances Martha BRAY
b. 1864
d. 1923

Mar.

Anne
b. 1837
d. 1927

Martha Pheobe
b. 1839
d. 1890

Jeremiah
b. 1842
d. 1847
drowned
Leekbrook

2 sons   1 daughter

Ellinor
b. 1865
d. 1947

Mildred Annie
b. 1867
d. 1958

Mar.

Ada Mary
b. 1873
d. 1956

Grace

George Herbert
b. 1874
d. aged
15 weeks

Francis
b. 1875
d. 1886

Elizabeth Leeke
b. 1877
d. 1946

Horace Townley
b. 1869
d. 1933

Mar.

Mary (Kitten)
b. 1862
d. 1935

Tom-Edmund
d. 1931

Herbert
b. 1859
d. aged
3 days

Anne
b. 1858
d. 1858

Mary
b. 1860
d. 1863

Gilbert Charles
b. 1862
d. 1943

Mar.

Arthur Henry
b. 1864
d. 1916

Mar.

Bernard
b. 1865
d. 1931

Mar.

Frederick Darlington Young
b. 1866
d.

Mar.

Lydia
b. 1868
d. 1949

Margaret Elizabeth
b. 1869
d. 1949

Mar.

Tom
b. 1871
d. 1925

Mar. 1900

Edith
b. 1872
d. 1925

Mar.

Gabrielle GUERET

Walter R. UNDERHILL
b. 1878
d. 1934

4 sons
1 daughter

Mary POPPLETON

Anne WELCH

2.Katherine FEARON
d. 1920

1.Mary Blanche CHALLINOR
d. 1920

Lucy
d. 1891

1.in 1889- Philip Jukes WORTHINGTON
d. 1902

2.in 1904- Sir Guy GAUNT
dissolved 1928

Lancelot Jukes

4 sons
1 daughter

Dorothy + ?

4 sons

John

daughter

daughter

Michael   Joan.

Thomas

Gilbert
d. 1940

Geoffrey
d. 1991

twins

INTRODUCTION

The author and publishers wish to acknowledge the help received from many sources in compiling this book. A full list of the original material consulted is listed at the end of the book (pages 179, 180), and thanks are expressed to the owners or custodians of this primary source material. A particular word of thanks is due to Leek Library, Nicholson Institute, Leek. The library holds a comprehensive collection of material relating to the Wardle family, including a large number of Thomas Wardle's published works - books, pamphlets and lectures - together with photographs, letters and other documents. The author and publishers are grateful to the Librarian for allowing free access to this material, much of which is reproduced within these pages.

The photographs on pages 68 and 69 are by courtesy of Mr.T.W.W.Jones. Photographs of Swainsley, the Wardles in court dress and those on pages 140, 141 and 142 are by courtesy of Mr.Philip Worthington. Mr.R.Poole has also contributed material from his collection.

Thomas Wardle's long and productive association with William Morris is given due consideration in the narrative, and the design forming the background to the front cover is Morris' MARIGOLD pattern, originally block-printed by Wardle.

Sir Thomas Wardle in later life.

Chapter One

EARLY DAYS

"FOR SILKEN FABRICS RICH AND RARE
WHAT CITIE CAN WITH LEEK COMPARE?"

So says the old Staffordshire ballad. But when Dr Johnson was writing to Mrs Thrale in 1773 he referred to "...Leek in the Moorlands, an old church but a poor town". In his day it was true. The population of Leek was under 4000 and button making was the main industry. A small market town, it was the centre of the remote Staffordshire Moorlands, where communications were poor, the countryside beautiful and farming a hard struggle for survival. When the industrial revolution came to Leek at the beginning of the nineteenth century, it changed Johnson's 'poor town' into the silk producing place of the ballad within the short space of fifty years. Together with Macclesfield and Congleton, Leek became part of the rich Midland group of silk manufacturing towns. From a mere eight silk works in 1807, it had 50 by 1870. Business thrived, and the population more than trebled, the swift progress of prosperity being due almost entirely to the silk trade.

There were fortunes to be made at this period of fast economic growth. One of the enterprising young men who made the most of the situation was Joshua Wardle. Although Wardle was a very common name in Leek, Joshua's branch of the family originated at Ipstones. His grandfather, also named Joshua, married a girl called Nancy Allen in 1809. She was a niece of Thomas Allen, a man of considerable substance in Macclesfield. Mr Allen was twice Mayor of the town, a J.P. and owned the Park Green Dye Works. This gentleman was spoken of as having 'sponsored' the Wardle family. They left Ipstones and settled in the Sutton area of Macclesfield. Joshua the elder and his son Joseph worked as stonemasons, while Joseph's son, young Joshua, was taken on at the Park Green Dye Works as an apprentice.

The dyeing of silk was a skilled and complicated process which required chemical knowledge as well as a plentiful supply of soft clean water. Joshua was quick to learn and very observant. By the time he was 27, he must have been confident that he had a sound knowledge of the work for he decided that he was ready to set up in business on his own. He had noticed for some time that a large amount of the silk sent to the Park Green works for dyeing came from Leek. The number of silk works there was increasing all the time, and Joshua reckoned that if he could start a dyeworks in Leek itself, there should be plenty of custom. Accordingly, on May 1st 1830, he went to Leek to look for a possible site.

A story about this visit was published in the Leek Times in 1980. It may be apocryphal, but it is certainly possible and worth repeating. On arrival, Joshua walked down the road in the direction of Cheddleton. He was looking for a place where there would be an abundant supply of soft, absolutely unpolluted water. He thought he had found what he was looking for, a small stream running to the south of Leek town. Walking back to the road he met a man who was on his way to the May Fair in Leek. They talked about the stream and Joshua's idea of starting a new dyeworks there, with the result that his new acquaintance led Joshua back down the road further towards Leekbrook, where there was a larger and much more suitable stretch of water. Delighted, Joshua decided at once to have his works there. By way of thanks to the stranger for his help, he straightway offered him a job. In one day, therefore, he had found both his site and his first employee. Negotiations for the buying of land must have been speedier than they are today, for by November the new dyeworks was in operation, just six months since Joshua had first seen the site.

Joshua's wife, Mary, (née Darlington) was expecting her first baby in January. She remained in Macclesfield while Joshua built a house for them across the road from the dyeworks, at Cheddleton Heath. The baby, Thomas, was born on January 26th 1831, and baptised at St. George's Church, Macclesfield on February 23rd. When the baby was about three months old, he was taken to Cheddleton to join his father. White's Directory of 1834 describes the village thus: 'Cheddleton is a small village, pleasantly seated on an eminence above the Caldon Canal and the River Churnet. It is 3 miles South of Leek, comprising within its parish 1664 inhabitants, and the three townships of Cheddleton, Basford and Consall, the latter of which supports its poor separately and the other two conjointly.' Joshua's works and his house were listed under the Basford entry. 'Basford', continued the Directory, 'is 3½ miles South by East of Leek, a hamlet and manor, of which William Sneyd, Esq., is lord.'

The new dyeworks had plenty of custom, as Joshua had foreseen. Silk from Leek and from much further afield was brought to be dyed on the bankside in large copper cauldrons which were filled with stream water and heated by charcoal fires beneath them. When the dyeing of the skeins was done, they were washed off, again in the stream water. Although there was plenty of silk to be dyed, there was not plenty of money, and Joshua found himself unable to expand as he would have wished. Some of his early business papers are in the Staffordshire Record Office, and they show a constant struggle against debtors who delayed payment and creditors who demanded it. He had considerable quantities of silk stolen from his premises when he was just beginning to make headway, and this incurred a big loss for him and heavy solicitor's fees. There were many complaints from customers about late deliveries among the correspondence, which could have been avoided if he had been able to employ more workers. The lateness of his own supplies also aggravated the situation. Most of his supplies were brought by the Shardlow Boat Company to Cheddleton Wharf by canal. There was soap from

Manchester, Fuller's Earth from Hull, soda and 'valonia' from Liverpool, Orchil and Cudbear from Bethnal Green, victriol from Birmingham, bricks from the Shelton Brick Works, many chemicals from Macclesfield and coal, which was purchased locally. In addition, there were carriage costs to be paid; with a carter charging as much as 10/- a day and an annual saddler's bill of £3.1.4, these were considerable extra expenses about which he complained bitterly.

Joshua had retained his business interests in Macclesfield, with a man called Thorley acting as his agent. In 1834 Thorley sent him a bill:

Rent of dyehouse..........£11.5.0
Rent of house.............£2.10.0
Interest on bill...........£1.0.0
Cash......................£59.0.0

Joshua's mother still lived in the house in question, and he continued to pay her rent of £2.10.0 per quarter for the rest of her life, though often in arrears. The interest and the cash loan show that he was still struggling financially, and for the next few years he was frequently indebted to Thorley who often protested that he could not afford long credit. Within seven years of starting the new works, Joshua bought more land from a Mr Brough. His initial money problems were over, the business was expanding and he needed more stream rights. There was even more incentive now to make a success of his business as his family had been increasing at two yearly intervals. By 1839, Thomas the eldest had been joined by Elizabeth, George, Anne and Phoebe. (Later Joshua and Mary had another son, Jeremiah, but he was drowned in Leekbrook at the age of five).

Thomas, naturally, was destined for the dyeworks. His father saw with pride that his eldest son was lively and intelligent, and was determined to give him as good an education as possible, and certainly better than he himself had had. When he was old enough, Thomas was sent to the Birch Grove Academy in Macclesfield as a boarder. It must have been hard to be separated from his brothers and sisters, but his grandmother was still in Macclesfield so perhaps he was allowed to see her sometimes. Among Joshua's business papers is a letter from Thomas, aged 10, marked by his father "arrived by accident". As was common in 1841, it was a thick piece of paper, folded and sealed without an envelope. The writing was beautiful, regular copperplate even at that age, while the contents were a typical schoolboy's letter:

"My dear Father and Mother, It is with pleasure that I write to you and trust it finds you in good health as it leaves me. The holidays are just approaching.....and I shall be very happy to see you all at home." After a lengthy description of various sermons he had heard, it ends by sending the regards of the headmaster to his parents, "and with my own love to you all, I remain, Your affectionate son, Thomas Wardle."

For that Victorian period, it was a warm and lively letter from a child to his parents. There were two terms a year at Birch Grove, with only short holidays in between. A school bill for Thomas has survived, showing that it cost Joshua £17.11.0 for half a year's board and tuition. (See Appendix 1). Thomas seems to have been happy at school. He made friends easily all his life, and took trouble to keep in touch with them. One friend he made at Birch Grove was a boy called Charles Lowe. Over fifty years later he dedicated one of his books to Charles, and he kept up with the Lowe family right into his old age.

There was a brief spell when Thomas attended the old village school at Cheddleton. Years later, he described it as *"small and unsuitable in every way as such schools were in those days."* The final part of his education was at Leek Grammar School. This had been built by the Earl of Macclesfield in 1723; it was not endowed so the headmaster was responsible himself for any repairs. Consequently little had ever been done to maintain it. There were 24 pupils and it received a poor report from the Schools Enquiry Commission in 1868. Nevertheless, as there was no alternative in Leek at that time, it was where the sons of well-to-do parents were sent, and again Thomas made many lifelong friends while he was there. He is said to have left school early in order to enter his father's business. His friend William Brough left at the age of sixteen, so perhaps Thomas did likewise. Whatever the shortcomings of the Leek Grammar School, he left it with a boundless thirst for knowledge and enthusiasm for life.

During Thomas' years at school, Joshua's firm had prospered. He had taken a William Milner into a short term partnership in 1839, Milner buying himself into the business for £1000, The firm then became 'Joshua Wardle and Co.', but shortly after Thomas started work 'and Co.' changed to 'and Son'. Joshua put his son through all the departments of the works, making sure he had a sound practical knowledge of every process. He also entrusted Thomas with the task of travelling to Macclesfield every week to pay the wages to his employees at the dyeworks there.

A speciality at Macclesfield had been a raven black dye. When Joshua started to produce it at the Leek works, he brought it to perfection. Thomas spoke of it thus: *"The water of the river Churnet has for about a century been celebrated for its peculiar dyeing properties, being especially suitable for the dyeing of black silk. The raven black is well known throughout the country. It is so-called from its similarity of hue to the rich blue-black plumage of the raven, whose bluest feathers are only rivalled by this celebrated dye. It is the bluest black in the world, and is only produced at Leek, other centres of the silk industry having tried in vain to rival it."* What was more, it could withstand boiling, did not bleach with exposure to light, and actually darkened with age. Considering the amount of black worn by Victorians, no wonder it was popular!

Joshua was interested in all aspects of the silk industry; the more variety of floss, the more there was for him to dye. One of the Indian wild silks, tussur, presented a challenge, being peculiarly intractable to dye. Even before Thomas had joined his father in the firm, Joshua had tried to solve the problem of tussur. If he had succeeded, there would have been a whole species of previously unusable silk available to the manufacturers, and silk imports into the country could have been doubled. Despite all his experience and chemical skill, Joshua was not successful with his experiments. Later, Thomas remembered his father's efforts when he himself tried to conquer this difficult silk.

For the next ten years, Thomas worked for his father. His brother George, who was four years younger, joined him, and the firm became 'Wardle and Sons'. There were great changes in the manufacturing side of the silk industry during these years. For fifty years there had been no competition from abroad as foreign manufactured silk imports had been banned. The heart of the English silk industry was at Spitalfields, in London, many of the workers being refugee French Huguenots. While the industry was developing and thriving in the provinces, the economic philosophy of the day was influenced by Cobden, the advocate of the doctrine of Free Trade. By 1824, the heavy duty on imported raw silk was abandoned, and on thrown silk it was halved. Shortly afterwards, manufactured silk goods were allowed into the country, although with a 35% duty. The effect on the English silk industry was two-fold: there was an increase in throwing mills, and a depression among the weavers. With the relaxation on imported goods, French silks immediately became popular, notwithstanding the duty. There was nothing amiss in the quality of the weaving of the home-produced silks, but it was the superiority of the French design and colouring that made them more popular. The English manufacturers, aware of this deficiency, were reluctant to display their products at the Great Exhibition in 1851. After persuasion, they agreed to put on a small exhibition of English silks, but they were not anxious to be compared unfavourably with the French. In 1860, the final blow fell: the Royal Speech at the opening of Parliament in January announced a commercial treaty with France (Palmerston was the Prime Minister and Gladstone the Chancellor).

The prevailing current of opinion throughout the country as well as in Parliament itself was in favour of Free Trade, so the treaty was welcomed in most quarters. Articles in the Times explained the implications of the proposal: French cotton, woollen and silk goods were to be duty free. A despairing letter to the paper from the Rector of St. Matthew's, Bethnal Green, told of the desperate poverty of the poor silk weavers who were unemployed in his parish. Some had been forced to change their occupations to unskilled jobs where they could barely scrape a living, some emigrated to America, some less fortunate ones died in the workhouse, and not a few committed suicide from despair and wretchedness. A silk lobby did put an amendment to the House of Commons which would have excluded silk goods from the treaty, but it was defeated. Gladstone was reputed to have said,

"Let the silk trade perish and go to the countries where it properly belongs". Since the English climate was not suitable for the rearing of silk worms, raw silk had always to be imported, whether from France, Italy, India or the Far East. But when it came to throwing, twisting, spinning and weaving, then the English climate had proved itself to be eminently suitable for those purposes.

Cossetted in the past by the ban on foreign imports for so many years, the home industry did not stand up well to foreign competition. In Leek, however, the silk trade was still booming. By 1850, there were over 4000 persons employed in the silk industry, many of them being women and girls. Winding and doubling were carried on in small workshops and cottage homes, where families worked 12-13 hours a day. Out-twisters would often employ 5-6 others, many of them children. The Wardle brothers found themselves in a business that was still expanding, with no shortage of custom, but they must have been aware that decline was threatening the manufacturers and that would also affect the dyers. But as it was, the Wardle reputation was high. Thomas had become even more proficient than his father at the chemical side of the work. He was passionately interested in chemistry and kept himself abreast of all the latest developments by reading all the technical publications he could lay hands on. In fact, all his life he was to be an avid reader of scientific journals and reports.

Meanwhile at home, all the family shared a love of music, with Thomas and his youngest sister, Phoebe, being particularly talented. Accustomed to singing and enjoying music at home, the family found their weekly worship at Cheddleton Church very frustrating. The hymns were sung by the sexton accompanying himself in the gallery on a barrel organ, which had a twenty tune capacity. Morning service always began with 'Awake my soul and with the sun...', and in the evening with 'Glory to Thee my God this night...'. And this comprised the whole musical content of the services for years. Thomas was one of a deputation who plucked up courage to go to the Vicar, the Rev.E.Powys, to ask for a more extended musical programme. The Reverend's reply was that he needed to keep the services short as he did duty at three churches each Sunday a long way apart, but the congregation could stay on and sing after the service if they liked. As may be imagined, this reply far from satisfied the music-loving Wardles, but their opportunity came when a new Vicar was appointed. With his blessing a choir was formed, which included both Thomas and his brother George. The sexton and the barrel organ were displaced by the enthusiastic new choir, of which Thomas was the first choirmaster; he led their practice on a concertina. To their great pride, they became the first surpliced choir in the Cheadle Rural Deanery. The Lichfield Diocesan Choral Association was established in 1856, 'to promote and improve congregational singing in the Churches in the Diocese'. According to the minutes, 'the origin of the movement is traced to a few parishes in the neighbourhood of Cheadle, which was organised for the improvement of choirs in that district.'

Having attained some proficiency in choral music, a united effort was made and general gatherings were held, one of which in the fine church of Leigh, produced so grand an effect as to suggest an even larger meeting. That year 27 choirs met together for a music festival, by the next year there were 47. Seven hundred singers met in Lichfield Cathedral on that occasion. A special train was run for the day, and complicated arrangements had to be made for refreshments. The Cheddleton choir attended festivals in 1856, 1857, 1861 and 1862. This indeed was progress from the days of the sexton and the barrel organ. The movement, which had certainly been stimulated in the Cheadle deanery by Thomas' efforts, had become an important diocesan activity.

St. Edward's Church in Leek (known as the old Parish Church) was the scene of one of the major events of Thomas' life. In 1857, he married a distant cousin, Elizabeth Wardle, three years younger than himself. Her father, Hugh Wardle, came of yeoman stock from Bradnop and Cheddleton (though on her brother's marriage certificate, Hugh's profession was given as 'druggist'). Her mother belonged to the well known local family of Leeke. She had been educated at Stone, Oulton and Codsall, so she, like Thomas, had been sent away to school. Thomas had chosen a bride who was intelligent, loyal, artistic and with an outstanding organising ability (of which he was probably not aware at that point).

The young couple lived at Leekbrook, either with Joshua and Mary or else in one of the neighbouring houses which belonged to them. Thomas became a churchwarden, and when a Sunday School was started by the new Vicar, he and Elizabeth taught in it, together with his brother George and his sisters, Anne and Phoebe. Life in Victorian times was very much centred on church affairs. Although Joshua and Mary were not much involved in parish activities, their family made up for it. After a year, a baby (Annie) was born to Thomas and Elizabeth, but she did not survive. Their second child, Herbert, was baptised at Cheddleton but only lived a few days. When Mary was born the following year, their joy was all the greater after the sorrow of losing their first two children.

The next family event was the marriage of Elizabeth's brother, George Young Wardle. Like his sister, he was both artistic and practical. He had left his home town of Leek to earn his living as a drawing master in Plymouth. While he was there, he met and fell in love with a young Scottish woman, Madeleine Hamilton Smith. To begin with, he apparently did not connect her with the notorious Madeleine Smith who not long previously had stood trial for the murder of her lover by arsenic poisoning. The trial had been a real *cause celebre*, with publicity that shocked the whole newspaper-reading public. It was extraordinary enough for a young middle class lady to have a lover and to be accused of murder, but what caused extra public outrage was the blatantly sexual content of the correspondence read out in court from Madeleine to her lover. Some of the most shocking parts were omitted, but this was all the more titillating. In those days, defendants had to be present in court throughout their trial, but were not allowed to speak in their own defence. Madeleine was an extremely attractive young woman, very well dressed and behaved with complete composure throughout. She evidently impressed the jury for they brought in a verdict of 'Not proven', leaving Madeleine's guilt or innocence unresolved. Suspicion remained in everyone's minds, and her family suffered deeply long after the trial was over. Her disillusioned fiance married someone else, and Madeleine decided to start a new life in London. She had an allowance from her father, she was still young and attractive, so a break from her past seemed the best step.

Before settling in London, she went to Plymouth to pay a visit to a clergyman friend, and it was during this visit that she met George Wardle. Her clerical friend watched the blossoming romance with misgivings, and finally considered it his duty to tell George her identity. Whether George was convinced of her innocence, or whether he was too much in love to care, the revelation made no difference. They became engaged and decided to settle in London. The marriage took place at St. Paul's, Knightsbridge, on July 4th, 1861. Madeleine's father travelled South to give her away, and made a generous settlement on her. It is not recorded whether George's sister Elizabeth and her husband Thomas went to London for the wedding, or whether they knew her past history, but they maintained a close relationship with George.

1862 and 1863 were eventful years. Another little Wardle was born, Gilbert Charles; Thomas gave his first public lecture, and wrote his first published work. The lecture was one of a winter series arranged by the Vicar of Leek on the subject of coal. The first part of the lecture dealt with the geological properties of coal, with many samples on display. The second was concerned with various derivatives of coal tar. Starting with gases, Thomas went on to explain the methods by which dyes were obtained from benzol. New shades of mauve, magenta and purple were now available from chemical sources, and he showed a yellow dye not previously seen in public, 'aurine', recently developed by his old school friend Charles Lowe, who by now was a research chemist. Taking care to explain methods of dyeing silk, Thomas gave high praise to the colours produced by the new chemical, or aniline, dyes. This was ironic considering that much of his fame as a dyer in later life came from his revival of the old natural vegetable-based dyes. It must have been an expensive lecture for him, with a large number of exhibits to prepare, but he was thorough by nature and was anxious to create a good impression. This he certainly did, the local paper reporting the lecture as having been 'exceedingly instructive, the attention of the audience being very marked'.

The first part of the lecture brought to the fore the knowledge Thomas had gained from his favourite hobby, geology. All his life he had loved the moorlands round Leek, spending many hours walking and looking for fossils. He must have been self taught, but his reading on the subject was wide and he was surrounded by perfect country for collecting specimens. Among his Leek acquaintances, he must have already made a name as an amateur geologist, because when John Sleigh wrote his definitive study on the history of Leek, it was Thomas whom he asked to write the chapter on the local geology. Published in 1862, the book had the title 'History of the Ancient Parish of Leek in Staffordshire, by John Sleigh (of the Inner Temple, Barrister-at-Law), with a chapter on the geology of the neighbourhood by Thomas Wardle of Leekbrook'. In fact, Thomas' contribution amounted to one-fifth of the whole book. He enlisted the help of his brother-in-law George Young Wardle to draw the fossils for some of the illustrations, recording his thanks to him among the credits. The town of Leek stands partly on Millstone Grit to the East, and partly on New Red Sandstone, or Middle Triassic. The carboniferous limestone which abounds in the neighbourhood had various industrial uses such as building stone and fireclay. All this Thomas described in detail, adding many local touches which lightened the academic content: *"The Churnet Valley has recently been found to have a rich vein of iron ore with good smelting qualities, not needing previous drying or calcining"*.

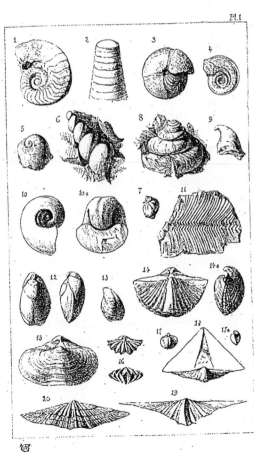

Pl.1

EXPLANATION OF THE PLATES.

The fractions show the number of times or diameters the figures are reduced or enlarged.

PLATE I.

CEPHALOPODA.

1.	Nautilus ; Discites sulcatulus, *Phillips*, ¼ . . .	Wetton Hill.
2.	Orthoceras Breynii, *Martin*, ⅔	Alstonfield.
3.	Goniatites sphæricus, *Martin*, ½	Alstonfield.
4.	Goniatites rotiformis, *Phillips*	Wetton.

GASTEROPODA.

5.	Natica ampliata, *Phillips*	Dove-dale.
6.	Murchisonia, probably tæniata, (cast) *Verneuil* . .	Caldon Low.
7.	Turbo biserialis, *Phillips*	Gateham.
8.	Euomphalus rotundatus, *Sowerby*	Wetton Hill.
9.	Pileopsis tubifer, *Phillips*	Gateham.
10.	Bellerophon apertus, *Sowerby* (cast) ½	Caldon Low.
10A.	„ „ front view.	

PTEROPODA.

11.	Conularia quadrisulcata (fragment) *Sowerby* . . .	Gateham.

BRACHIOPODA.

12.	Terebratula hastata, *Sowerby*, front and side views	Beeston Tor.
13.	„ vesicularis, *De Koninck*	Wetton.
14.	Spirifera trigonalis, variety bisulcata, *Sowerby*, dorsal valve and hinge-line, (common).	
14A.	„ „ „ side view.	
15.	„ elliptica, *Phillips*, ⅔	
16.	„ octoplicata, *Sowerby*, front and anterior views.	
17.	„ Urii, *Fleming*, dorsal valve	Wetton Hill.
17A.	„ „ „ side view.	
18.	„ cuspidata, *Martin*, ¼	Wetton Hill.
19.	„ triangularis, *Martin*, remarkable variety .	Gateham.
20.	Cyrtina septosa, *Phillips*	Valley of the Dove.

From Sleigh's History of Leek (1862)

Mentioning the Potteries and Cheadle coalfield, he said, *"The precise conditions which contributed to the conversion of vegetable matter into coal, and to the formation of coal measures, are as yet imperfectly understood."* Thomas never pretended he had knowledge he did not possess; he was intellectually honest, and always gave due credit to his sources of information. Another quotation from his chapter: *"In the lower part of Stockwell Street, Leek, when the deep sewer was being made in 1861, I observed, in the shales which were being thrown to the surface, several shells of the genus Cardiomorpha, and also plants".*

 Always observant, he found geological points of interest everywhere. He listed analyses of all the local water and springs, which must in part have been compiled from knowledge due to his dyeing expertise. The alum springs of Wall Grange, for instance, one mile from Leek, he recorded as having water so red in hue that the 'poor people of old' used to dye their button-moulds with it. He advised his readers that the best place to look for mountain limestone fossils was from the Waste and Kniveden quarries near the Buxton Road toll bar, one mile from Leek. He ended by suggesting that a geological museum be established in Leek, connected with the Literary and Mechanics Institute. It would encourage the young to walk and enjoy the scenery, *"The writer can add from experience that the hammer is no mean companion to the walking stick. So many interesting specimens could be found locally that a really good collection could be made, which would be educational for all."* The information in the chapter was well received. Thomas had made a scholarly report, had done research for it, and given comprehensive lists, diagrams and analyses. As a result of this work he was put up for membership of the Geological Society, and was elected a Fellow the following January, 1863. He was always extremely proud of his Fellowship, as his family must also have been. The suggestion of a geological museum was not taken up, but in due course Thomas gave his own splendid collection of fossils to the town of Leek.

The year that started so well with the geological Fellowship ended with tragedy for Thomas and Elizabeth. Their beloved little Mary died that December, aged three. She was buried in Cheddleton churchyard, beside her baby brother and sister. It must have been a particular ordeal for Elizabeth as she was seven months pregnant with her next child. Thomas presented a new bell to the church in memory of Mary, "a beloved daughter, my eldest child". It was inscribed – 'And children's voices echo making answer Alleluia'. Two other new bells had recently been given by the parishioners to mark the reconstruction of the church, so Cheddleton then had a full peal.

Sir Gilbert Scott and his son had undertaken the major restoration of the church, in which Thomas as church warden had been much involved. At one point, he had a disagreement over one of the thirteenth century columns in the nave with a fellow church warden, who wanted to have it removed because it did not match the others. *"But,"* wrote Thomas afterwards, *"I thought history of more importance than correspondence of moulding, and I think I saved it; but it took a great architect and an Archdeacon to help me, and my colleague gracefully gave way"*. The work took the best part of two years, all the parishioners having subscribed a considerable sum for the purpose. As well as the bell, Thomas gave one hundred hymn books for the congregation and paid for the restoration of a broken fourteenth century cross in the churchyard. New embroideries having been designed by the architect for the restored church, Elizabeth gave and worked some alms bags and was involved with other ladies of the parish in working the altar furnishings. Her sisters-in-law gave and worked the sedilia cushions, George gave books for the choir and his newly-wed wife sewed a bookmark and promised a carpet for the pulpit stairs. At the reopening ceremony, the local paper reported that the Bishop and thirty clergy were present, the choristers were conducted by Mr T Wardle, while 'the congregation joined in more generally and heartily in both the singing and the responses than is, unfortunately, at all customary in this district'. Cheddleton parishioners must have been very pleased to read such praise. They certainly had a restored church of which they could be very proud.

An interesting point was that Morris and Co. had executed several of the windows, and William Morris must have visited Cheddleton in person for he is known to have made favourable comment on three angels by Burne-Jones in one of the South aisle windows. He was responsible for the design of the two side pieces of the altar triptych, and also of the carvings on the new shaft of the old cross in the churchyard. He must, therefore, have met the Wardles before his celebrated visits to the dyeworks, and before George Young Wardle went to work for him.

Two Wardle weddings took place in Cheddleton church in the course of the year: George married Frances Martha Bray in July, shortly before the official reopening, and Thomas' eldest sister, Elizabeth, married John Illsley, brewer, in November. Earlier, Thomas and Elizabeth's new baby had been christened Arthur Henry in the new alabaster font which had just been presented by a benefactress from Leek.

During this time of family happenings and involvement in church affairs, the business of Joshua Wardle and Sons was still doing well, and was using the new aniline dyes almost exclusively. They were cheaper and easier, the colours were brighter than the old ones, though at first they tended to be fugitive - that is, they were not fast and faded unevenly. The Wardle expertise soon overcame these problems and the chemical dyes were used satisfactorily. The best silk was brought to them for dyeing before being woven, but the cheaper products were dyed 'in the piece'. George was now experienced in all the processes as well as Thomas, and the two of them could have run the works on their own, but Joshua was not ready to hand over. His two sons were very different: George was a plodder, reliable and willing, while Thomas was impatient and ambitious. He foresaw that difficult times were ahead and wanted to diversify into the printing and finishing sides of the industry, a suggestion not acceptable to his father. Joshua may well have been irritated by his elder son's increasingly dominant personality, and by his interests outside the firm. At the age of thirty, Thomas could already put the letters F.G.S. (Fellow of the Geological Society) after his name, whereas Joshua at the same age had been far too busy building up the business to be able to indulge in outside pursuits.

Whatever the reasons for their decision, in 1866 Thomas and Elizabeth moved into Leek itself with their increasing family. They now had four boys, Bernard and Frederick Darlington having been born within the two previous years. They settled in St. Edward Street (formerly Spout Street), at number 62, a grey stone house built in 1724, with Tudor style windows and a curious spouthead decorating the front. It must have been a wrench to leave Leekbrook and the rest of the family, also to move away from Cheddleton into another parish. But there were compensations in living in the town itself, not least being more independent. After the move, the family worshipped at St. Edward's Church in Leek, just up the road from their home. Thomas in no way deserted his interest in church music. He assisted the St. Edward's choir from time to time, and later played the harmonium for services held at the All Saints' school and at the Ball Haye mission room. He was on the Deanery Music Committee for Leek, and made sure that the Leek churches, as well as Cheddleton, entered their choirs for the Diocesan festivals, which were now held every three years.

Shortly before the move from Cheddleton, the North Staffordshire Field Club and Archaelogical Society was formed. At its first Annual General Meeting in Stoke-on-Trent in 1866, 117 members were listed including Mr T Wardle of Leekbrook. The activities of the club were of absorbing interest to him, and he remained a member all his life. He made many new acquaintances with similar interests, enjoyed the expeditions and spent many hours preparing papers when invited to address the meetings. After only three years, he was elected one of the vice-presidents. That year he read a scholarly paper on the geology of the Roches, a local rocky outcrop where the club had visited on their Summer expedition. The committee thought so highly of his address that they insisted it should be published.

The next few years saw more increases to the Wardle family. George and his wife, Frances Martha (née Bray) had five children in quick succession: Ellinor, Mildred Anne, Horace, Ada and Grace. Ellinor, or Nellie as she was known, became a great favourite with her aunt and uncle. Elizabeth's next two babies were both girls: Lydia Young, who grew up to be her mother's right-hand girl, and Margaret Elizabeth, the beauty of the family, with her father's lively, impulsive temperament.

Meanwhile, George Young Wardle and Madeleine had settled in Bloomsbury in London. He worked as a draughtsman and became well regarded in artistic circles. Madeleine bore him two children, a girl known as Kitten and a son called Tom. They were on the fringes of the pre-Raphaelite set for some years, which may account for him receiving several commissions from William Morris. When Morris took him on as manager to his firm in 1870, it was not only the start of a business relationship but also of a long and sincere friendship. Madeleine fitted very happily into the artistic circle in which they now moved. She entertained a lot in their house in Bloomsbury, becoming friendly with Janie Morris and her sister, Elizabeth Burden. She enjoyed their company and their Socialist principles, being of 'avant garde' taste herself. She took up water colour painting quite successfully, and also used to help with the Morris embroideries. Whether her new acquaintances knew of her past history or not, they did not let it make any difference to their friendship with the Wardles.

Six years passed since Thomas and family had moved away from Leekbrook, and Joshua was now nearly seventy. One last crisis hit the firm: the silk workers' strike. There had been discontent for some time over wages. As early as 1853, the Leek silk twisters had formed a Society and succeeded in getting a small rise, so that by the 1860's they were earning 18/- a week. Two hundred of them paid 30/- a year to belong to the Society, which was quite a high proportion of their wages. The silk employers were paternalistic towards their workers. There were outings for the families and treats for the children, but trade unions were very much frowned upon. In 1871, the trimming weavers formed another Society, staged a small strike and won their wage claim. It was a small affair and soon resolved, but it unsettled the dyers. The moderate success of the trimming weavers encouraged them to take similar action. The next January, both Hammersley's and Wardle's dismissed twenty one men for wanting to join a Dyers' Society. When their colleagues threatened to strike in sympathy, the two firms agreed to reinstate the men as long as the Leek Dyers' Society was independent and not associated with Unions in other towns. That could have been the end of the matter, but one of the silk manufacturing firms almost immediately announced a reduction of working hours, to nine hours daily. Naturally, workers in all the other firms then wanted the same. The various employers decided to form their own association, and not to act independently of each other in future. They realised that a mild concern for their workers was not sufficient, and that new problems needed a serious and combined approach. The dyers asked for a 10% rise in wages, but when that was refused, they went on strike, putting their claim up to 20% plus a ¼ rate for overtime, bringing them in line with dyers' pay in other towns.

According to the Leek Times, 140 men turned out from four dyeworks though not from Wardles, so *'a procession went in orderly and quiet manner towards Leekbrook, with the result that all except twenty-five men from Wardles turned out.'* Twisters, pickers and women joined them until 3600 people were either on strike or locked out, and this lasted from February until April. Joshua Wardle wrote to the paper in March: *"....with regard to an increase in wages, in February we suggested to our men that they should elect a committee out of their members and we would discuss with them the practicability of an improvement. They voted a committee of eight of the most trustworthy and reasonable men in our employ."* This committee had moderate demands, but *"the demon of Trade Union onesidedness now seems to have gained the ascendant in the majority of our younger men and they broke away from their first arrangement and assailed the committee which had so faithfully represented their interests with epithets we will not repeat here. Our last communication from their Trade Union secretary, a man knowing nothing of the requirements or details of the trade, was an insolent demand for an impossible advance in wages."* He went on to say he had questioned many workers, both those on strike and those who were still working, and all agreed that their leaders were asking far more than they had wished them to do.

The dyers had hoped that kindred societies from other towns would help them, but they were already committed to supporting the dyers in Leicester who had been out on strike for some time. There were several very angry letters in the Leek Post, one accusing Joshua of advising the shopkeepers to give no credit, and another protest signed *"..from one who dyes to live".* Slowly, the heart went out of the struggle as the hardship to the strikers' families increased. When the employers announced a 10% rise for everyone and that the factories would be open again the following week, the workers drifted back to work. It had been a worrying time for Joshua, with work held up for three months, but once everything had settled down, there was to be peace in the Leek silk works for the next forty years or so.

Joshua apparently handled the strike himself, though presumably he consulted with his sons. It may have hastened his decision to hand over the business to them, for soon afterwards the Post Office directory lists Thomas and George as the silk dyers of Leekbrook, with Joshua only given among the residents of Cheddleton Heath. He continued to live there with Mary and their two unmarried daughters until he died.

The Presentation Clock

The workers at Leekbrook gave Joshua as a leaving present a very handsome pair of candlesticks and a French Ormolu China clock. The clock remained in family ownership but the candlesticks were given away.

BEECH GROVE ACADEMY,

MACCLESFIELD, 1844.

Mr Wardle

TO W. WATSON, Dec 16th

	£	s.	d.
For one Half Year's Board and Education of Master Thomas	15	"	"
Stationary, 10/- Use of Books and Maps 3/-	"	13	"
Drawing Book and Pencils	"	4	"
1 a/c Book	"	3	6
Books 1 Lat Grammar 2/ 1 Cat.m 1/6	"	3	6
1 England 1/10 1 Arith.c 2/6	"	3	4
Washing 1 Map 1/6 Collections 2/-	"	2	6
Shoe Maker's Bill 6/4 Quilling 5/-	"	11	4
Tailor's Bill 1/6 Seat in Chapel 2/6	"	3	"
Hair Cutting 1/ 1 Exercise Book 1/6	"	1	6
Paint Brush	"	"	7
2 Fronts 3/4 Clothes Brush 2/3	"	5	7
	£17	11	10

Settled, William Watson
Dec 19th 1844.
School will be Re-opened Jan 2nd

MASTER THOMAS WARDLE'S SCHOOL BILL
Beech Grove Academy, Macclesfield. Headmaster, William Watson
ONE HALF YEAR (1844) £17-11-10

Mrs. Joshua Wardle,
neé Mary Darlington

Cousin Mildred Wardle,
sister of Horace Wardle,
of Leekbrook

W.R.Kean   -The Grammar School-

The Old Leek Grammar School, attended by the young Thomas Wardle

St Edward's Church, Cheddleton

St Edward's Church, Leek, where Thomas and Elizabeth married in 1857

The Burne-Jones Window in St Edward's Church, Cheddleton

Old St Edward Stret, Leek - home of the Wardles for many years.

An early view of the Leekbrook factory

The Leekbrook factory today

Chapter Two

TUSSUR

Tussur silk, which had been such a disappointment to Joshua in his efforts to bleach and dye it, remained a challenge to Thomas. He kept the results of his father's experiments, determined one day to succeed himself. In 1860, he had read a detailed report by Dr Birdwood of the Bombay museum about the native Indian uses of tussur, recommending it to English manufacturers as having great commercial potential if only it could be developed. This reinforced Joshua's opinion, and encouraged Thomas to continue the research.

Tussur was named after the Sanskrit word for a shuttle: 'tasara', which the cocoon was supposed to resemble in shape. Other forms of the word were Tusser, Tasar, Tussah and Tussore; nowadays it is best known by this last name. As Thomas himself used the form 'Tussur', that form has been used throughout this work. It is the product of the Antheroea Mylitta moth, which abounds in the forests of India and feeds on the leaves of a variety of trees. The fully grown larva, or worm, is about four inches long with twelve joints or articulations in its body – green with reddish spots. The larva spins a cocoon approximately two inches long and one and a quarter inches in diameter, with a case so hard that a sharp knife has to be used to open it. It attaches the cocoon to the twigs of its host tree by a pedicle (or peduncle), which means that the supporting twig is encircled with a strong silken loop from which the cocoon is suspended by a silken stalk.

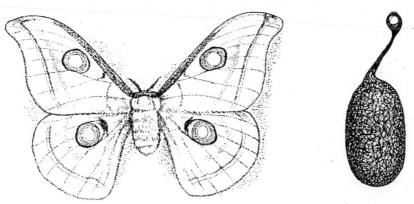

Antheraea mylitta, an Indian silk moth and its cocoon

The pedicle prevents the cocoon from falling while the chrsysalis inside is 'sleeping' for several months. When the imago (fully developed moth) is ready to emerge, it first emits a fluid which softens the hard outer case, and then parts the silk fibres at one end with its wing spines and legs until the hole is large enough for it to crawl out. This, of course, damages the fibres and would make it impossible to reel, so the cocoons are gathered when the worm inside has stopped spinning. By listening carefully, the spinning can be heard quite distinctly. Silence means that the worm has 'seriposited' all its silk. The female cocoons are larger and more regular than the male ones, so sufficient females can be identified and left to ensure the next supply of eggs. This moth crops once, and sometimes twice, a year. Tussur silk fibres are flat, one seven-hundred-and-fiftieth of an inch wide(0.034mm). Seen under a microscope, the thread consists of twenty or more smaller fibres, or fibrillae, lying side by side, joined by a resinous gum called 'sericin'. The natural colour of tussur is deep fawn. It had been used for centuries in India and elsewhere in its natural shade, but was very coarse silk, inclined, though not intended, to be 'slubbed'. It was very resistant to bleaching and impervious to normal dyeing process, while the hardness of the cocoon's outer case and the amount of gum coating the fibres made it difficult to reel smoothly. A further problem was that the flatness of the thread produced scintillations that made the colour look uneven.

Before he could start bleaching and dyeing, Thomas had to examine the fibres microscopically and discover a method of dissolving the protective gum. This was a lengthy process, and he could only work on it when his normal workload allowed the time. Gradually he made progress, firstly in the bleaching, increasing his knowledge of the fibres. He also improved the application of mordants in the dyeing, (a mordant is the substance which fixes the dye, by allowing it to penetrate the fabric). He first managed to produce greys of various shades, then primary colours in weak tones. Finally, by 1872, he managed to obtain a good yellow on tussur, a pale blue, red and tertiary hues. His years of work had finally been rewarded. What was more, he had acquired a good general knowledge of sericulture (i.e. cultivation of silk) far greater than that of the normal dyer, which was to be of much importance to him later in his career.

The future commercial use of tussur was his next concern. It was vital that the manufacturers should see it and wish to buy and use it. He realised, however, that one drawback to its economic viability was the large amount of waste that could not be used for weaving. The outer filaments of the cocoons came away in small pieces, only the inner part could be reeled into one long thread. Thomas wanted to find a use for this waste before trying to promote tussur to the silk manufacturers. He was sure that the waste could be used to produce a short pile fabric similar to velvet. He dyed some of it black and took it to various firms asking for it to be made up as an experiment, but failed to interest any of them in the idea. With great initiative, Thomas took his tussur to Crefeld in Germany and there the first piece of short pile tussur fabric was produced. The names given to it varied from sealcloth, sealskin and sealette to plush and plumrose. Thomas returned home in triumph, well pleased with the new fabric for it was rich, soft and glossy.

The next stage was to publicise tussur in its new dyed state, together with the sealcloth. An ideal opportunity presented itself the following year at the 1873 International Exhibition at the South Kensington Museum in London.

Thomas and his brother George took a display of black and coloured tussur in skeins, with some specially woven lengths of silk to illustrate its properties. As they had hoped, their display created much interest in the silk trade. The Marquess of Salisbury, then Secretary of State for India, was one who saw it and was very impressed. Talking with Thomas about the dyes, he enquired if the Indians could now be taught to dye their own tussur using the native dyestuffs. Knowing how long it had taken to perfect the process himself, and that one of the reasons for his final success lay in the mordants he had used, Thomas said that before he could advise the Indian dyers he would need to study and experiment with their dyestuffs. *"I put my services at the disposal of Lord Salisbury, asking that a selection of dyestuffs from India be sent to me for my examination".* In due course, these were sent to him, in such quantities that he then complained he had nowhere to store them! He may not have realised when he offered to undertake the work what an immense labour it would prove to be. In fact, it took him over seven years, even with the help of an assistant, to produce his Blue Book on 'The Dyes and Tans of India'.

The year 1872 was important for Thomas not only because of the tussur discovery. The Hencroft works were purchased from Samuel Tatton, a dyer and sub-postmaster in Leek, who had built the works on the banks of the River Churnet some thirty years previously.

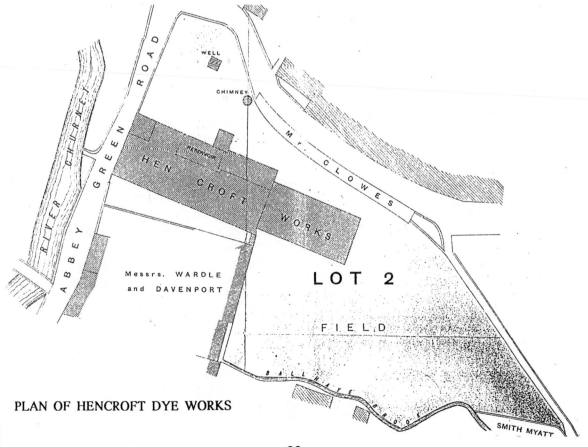

PLAN OF HENCROFT DYE WORKS

23

After a reservoir had been constructed at Tittesworth, the river water was adversely affected. It no longer ran clear constantly, but was muddy after rain, and was deteriorating progressively. It even became so bad that Samuel Tatton had to compensate some of his customers for damage to their silk. He sold the works to Thomas in 1872 for £3555, which was about half of what it would have been worth if the water had remained as clear as when he first built the works. Tatton stayed on as tenant for two or three years, so the acquisition of this new premises made no immediate difference to the work at Leekbrook. Having bought a property with a very imperfect water supply, Thomas must have had a good idea of what he proposed to do with it. In fact, when Samuel Tatton left, he used it for hand block printing. No doubt Joshua was disapproving of this seemingly unpromising venture, but the Hencroft works was later to be the scene of some of the firm's most outstanding achievements.

The other event of the year was one which gave Thomas great pleasure: he was elected President of the North Staffordshire Field Club for the year. He had been a very active Vice-President for three years, having arranged a number of expeditions as well as winter meetings at Leek. His friend William Brough was local secretary for Leek, and the two men worked well together to provide events of special interest for the ever-increasing membership. For his retiring presidential address, Thomas chose a geological subject: 'Limestone, its occurrence, nature and origin'. To illustrate his lecture, he had brought a display of mountain limestone fossils and trilobites from the Wenlock Silurian system. The text was published in the Field Club records and reads most interestingly. As before, he referred to various recent opinions appearing in the Geological Magazine and other journals. And when he came to put forward his own theory as to why certain limestone seems to be devoid of life forms, he introduced it with engaging modesty "...from my own observations, however imperfect and immature as they necessarily are". From the end of his presidential term, Thomas and William Brough were fellow Vice-Presidents for the next thirty five years or so, leading expeditions most years and reading papers to many of the Winter meetings. Thomas specialised, naturally, in geological and archaeological subjects, whereas Brough's interest was in botany, art and old books. At times, Thomas' enthusiasm may have been somewhat overwhelming for members; for instance, he led a party to the Marston old salt mine, and when they were in there he proceeded to read them "a thoroughly exhaustive paper on salt". Another expedition he led was not for the faint hearted, when they visited the Staffordshire Potteries Water Works and he lectured them about pure water supplies as they stood in the pouring rain. Whatever was his particular interest at the time, the Field Club would receive a paper on it. No matter how pressing were his business interests, he never grudged time spent preparing his work for the Field Club.

Tussur continued to occupy his attention. Although he had dyed it successfully, he was not satisfied with the texture. Deciding that he needed more knowledge of reeling and throwing techniques, he went out to Piedmont

24

in Italy, the chief station of the Italian silk industry. The silk normally processed at Piedmont was the the chief silk of commerce, the Bombyx Mori. Thomas had taken with him a supply of tussur cocoons and some raw silk for his experiments. At first, he was told it was 'pretty hopeless'. The Bombyx Mori cocoons were very much easier to unwind, only needing sufficient soaking in hot water for the silk fibres to be easily reeled. But the tussur ones were so hard that they needed to be boiled for a long time in water with glycerine, soap and potash. After this treatment, Thomas asked the most experienced girl to experiment with them. After taking the outer threads off, she managed to reel a cocoon almost without a break. Later he tried himself, and succeeded in unwinding a thread almost three-quarters of a mile long from a single tussur cocoon. He took careful note of the reeling equipment used in Piedmont, as the results were very much more even than any he had previously seen. Meanwhile, the raw silk he had taken to be thrown came out fine and entirely satisfactory.

The reelers themselves interested Thomas as well as their technical skills. He found they were of French origin, whose forbears had fled at the revocation of the Edict of Nantes, and had retained their own patois and old French songs. They worked from 5 am to 8 pm for one franc a day, then danced and sang for an hour before going to bed. Accommodation was provided for them at the factory for the reeling season, after which they dispersed to their Alpine villages.

Thomas returned home with the information he had sought, only to find Elizabeth grieving over the death of their latest child, George Herbert, who had only lived for fifteen weeks. This loss was followed shortly afterwards by the death of Mary, Thomas' mother, aged seventy one. Joshua continued to live at Cheddleton Heath with Anne and Phoebe, his unmarried daughters.

The success of dyeing tussur had made Thomas anxious for some recognition for his work in the chemical field. When two sponsors were willing to propose him, he was elected a Fellow of the Chemical Society in 1875, and had much pleasure in adding the letters F.C.S. after his name in future.

The Hencroft works became available when Samuel Tatton finally left, and Thomas lost no time in starting work there. The water must have cleared, because all the experiments on vegetable dyes with William Morris took place in one of the Hencroft vats. But it was intended for block printing, and after the Morris experiments were finished, it was turned over entirely to that.

A third dyeworks was acquired nearby, from Edward Smith, who had specialised in dyeing sewing silks. This was known as the Churnet Works, and later was called Sir Thomas and Arthur Wardle, advertising itself as doing finishing and printing, as well as dyeing.

The story of the association between Thomas and William Morris is told separately in chapter three. Sufficient to say here that the on-going work on

Indian dyes and tans made Thomas equally interested as Morris in the rediscovery of the methods of using natural dyestuffs.

Vegetable dyes were used for the tussur embroidery silks and for the most delicate work, but at Leekbrook the use of aniline dyes continued for economic reasons. To quote an article by Mabel Cox in 'The Artist' (1897): *'Mr Wardle has a separate works where he uses vegetable dyes, which are not commercially viable, but he does his own research into method and design. The smaller works are run for artistic reasons, and could not survive without the commercial success of the mass produced artificial dyes.'* She went on to list the advantages of the natural dyes:

> 1. *More beautiful lustrous colours "without that peculiar metallic appearance now alas, so familiar, and, we fear, so much admired."*
> 2. *They retain their relationships in artificial light.*
> 3. *They are more permanent.*
> 4. *Even when they do fade they do so artistically, all colours equally, thus retaining the balance of shades.*

"Mr Wardle," she continued, *"keeps an exposure book for cuttings of material which are exposed to strong sunlight, in which vegetable dyes stand the test better than the chemical ones, indeed, some of the latter are found to be absolutely colourless after twelve months' exposure".*

The range of work was now much greater, as Thomas had foreseen. From silks and cottons, Wardles went on to print cretonne, velveteen, velvet, woollen cloth and crepe de chine. Their reputation must have been high, for when Arthur Liberty started his new shop in Regent Street, it was they whom he asked to dye and print his Oriental fabrics. These included gauze from India, cashmere woollens, a very light tropical cotton and, of course, silks all kinds. Like William Morris, Liberty wanted to improve the nation's taste by providing beautiful things, but he did not go so far as to denounce all machine-made, mass produced goods as did Morris. He saw that handmade goods were too expensive except for luxury items, and could not be produced in sufficient quantity to satisfy the demand of the public. Liberty and Wardle combined to launch the new Art Colours, in delicate pastel tints. The windows of the Regent Street shop had white painted fretwork screens on which silks in Art Colours were draped in graduated shades. They became one of the sights of Regent Street, a revelation to a generation accustomed to harsh aniline dyes and to stiff silks and bombasines.

In the Wardle pattern books are examples of Mysore silks, corahs, tussurs, cottons and cotton velveteens, all either dyed or printed for Liberty's. Most designs were oriental but some were floral or allegorical by modern designers such as Walter Crane, Solon and Butterfield. Liberty had sold tussur silk from the outset for dresses and light furnishings in its natural colour, but as imported from India it only came in a narrow width. When it became available in colours and woven on a wider loom, Liberty found he had a product immensely admired by his customers and in great demand.

A letter has survived from this period written by Thomas from Leek to John Sleigh in London:

"I am trying to get off to the Geological dinner on Friday next. I have not been to one of their said-to-be Antediluvian feasts yet, but I am so busy dyeing and arranging the cases of three of our manufacturers who are exhibiting their wares at Philadelphia, I fear I cannot get off. If I can, I should very much like to come to you on Saturday afternoon and stay Sunday with it, if it is quite convenient. If I cannot finish my work here I will write to you postponing my visit a week or two. Yours very truly, Thomas Wardle. P.S. If you would like to go with me to the Geological Association, I should be delighted and we will dine with the Fellows and their friends."

He was obviously under considerable pressure at work, but it was a prestigious commission to be asked to dye fabrics for the international exhibition at Philadelphia. Thomas was gaining in social confidence, to be writing to a Barrister of the Inner Temple in such an informal manner and inviting him out to dinner. In fact, Thomas went to London quite frequently for business purposes, but he does not appear to have taken Elizabeth with him. She was much occupied organising the new embroidery work for the re-opening of Ipstones church after its restoration, and also with her increasing family. The last two babies were only a year apart: a son, Francis, and then her fourteenth and final child, a daughter called after her, Elizabeth Leeke. After this latter confinement, she became desperately ill and she had to leave the family home to be nursed by a girl employee, chosen by Thomas. She returned to Leekbrook, where she stayed with her sisters-in-law. With ten children now at 62 St. Edward Street she would not have had the absolute peace and quiet ordered by the doctor. Thomas visited her whenever he could. Even though they had servants, it was a time of great worry and difficulty having her away from home. It was a long illness, for two years later Thomas described her condition when writing to his brother in-law, George Y. Wardle: *"Lizzie is still very poorly but no worse, perhaps a shade better and a little stronger, though she cannot stand yet."* She did, however, make a full recovery and when she rejoined the family she came back to a new home. Their new house was only a few doors away, at 54 St, Edward Street, much larger, with a good garden and a tennis court. Thomas had bought it from Jacob Sykes, schoolmaster, for £1900. The office of Joshua Wardle and Sons and the Hencroft works occupied part of the premises, but there was plenty of room for the family as well. Six months after the above letter was written, Elizabeth, although not completely recovered, was well enough to start the Leek Embroidery Society (see Chapter Four).

During this period of family change and expanding business, Thomas found time for yet another outside interest, the Society for the Protection of Ancient Buildings. This was established in 1877 by William Morris. While he was visiting Leek, he and Thomas found they had very similar views on the need for a body to speak out against the widespread Victorian passion for demolition and wholesale restoration of old buildings. Thomas had already addressed the Field Club on the subject, criticising G.E.Street for *"the so-called restoration he was responsible for at Leek when a chancel with good fourteenth century windows on the South side and a well designed perpendicular East window were wiped out, to the loss of history and art work."* He had also waxed indignant over some of the restoration work at Cheddleton Church:

"...the church is of Millstone Grit, perhaps the best and most durable building stone in the country, except for some portion of the restored work, which was unfortunately done in the softer and less durable stone from the Triassic beds at Alton. The masons who wrought the church during its restoration were said to have strongly objected to work in the stone of the neighbourhood, owing to its hardness; and I suspect it cost the builder too much of his profit, as it doubtless took longer to do. I heard the builder say that tracery could not be wrought out of it, but that I proved to be a mistake, as you may see in the churchyard cross, which was wrought in London and is of Millstone Grit selected by myself from the Roaches and Wetley Rocks quarries. How sad it seems that while we possess such abundant stores of splendid building stone - stone which the ancient church builders of the south and south-west counties would have been delighted to meet with, in place of the oolitic sandstones and limestones, some of which are cut up by handsaws - people should be running miles away to fetch soft and easy cutting stone for works intended to last for centuries - stone that is neither suited to the humid climate nor possessing that durability for which Millstone Grit is noted."

Thomas was therefore entirely sympathetic to the aims and objects of the new Society and more than willing to throw himself into its campaign. He admired Morris for his intention never again to design and make windows for old churches except in very exceptional cases, for the most profitable part of Morris' business at that point was the church window work, and this was a considerable sacrifice.

The inaugural meeting in 1877 was only attended by ten people, one of them being Morris' manager and friend, George Y. Wardle. The following annual meeting was a very different scene: there were eighty members on the committee, including Thomas and his brother-in-law. Morris had used all his influence to gather people together with a common interest in ancient buildings; Burne-Jones, Holman Hunt, Ruskin, Alma Tadema, Coventry Patmore, Thomas Carlyle and the Bishop of Truro were among the distinguished names on the committee. By the following year, two new names are listed which may well have been recruited by Thomas: his friend William Brough from Leek, and Sir George Birdwood, who as Dr.Birdwood had encouraged Thomas in his tussur experiments. Thomas was made the local correspondent for Staffordshire. However, his first major battle concerned the proposed restoration scheme for Prestbury Church in Cheshire. He represented the Society at a meeting of the planning committee, but unfortunately antagonised his audience: firstly by trying to impress them by reading a long list of the important people who belonged to the Society, and secondly by criticising the architect, Sir Gilbert Scott. The people of Prestbury refused to be intimidated by the distinguished opposition to their restoration scheme, accused Thomas of not having read the proposals properly and reaffirmed their confidence in Sir Gilbert Scott. In retaliation, Thomas wrote a lengthy letter to the Macclesfield Courier which did nothing to pour oil on the troubled waters. Nevertheless, the minutes of the Society record that the Prestbury restoration committee had been influenced by their intervention and the scheme of repair 'much improved'.

To return to tussur, an International Exhibition was to be held in Paris in 1878, and Thomas was invited to be one of the Jurors for the Silk Section. This in itself was an honour, but he was even more excited by the fact that a collection of his tussur silks and sealcloth was to be shown by the express request of the President, the Prince of Wales. According to Thomas, it was Sir Philip Cunliffe-Owen of the South Kensington Museum who, having been very interested in the Wardle exhibit at South Kensington in 1873, drew the Prince's attention to the development of tussur silk. A display was carefully prepared consisting of hanks of bleached and dyed tussur silk yarns, and of woven and printed specimens, including the first piece of sealcloth. Thomas took it all to Paris and displayed it in the Silk Section. As he wrote afterwards: *"For this exhibit a Gold Medal was awarded to the Secretary of State for India. It was first awarded to me, but the exhibit being entirely of Indian tussur silk, I decided that it ought to go to the Secretary of State."* He went on: *"...as a member of the Silk Jury, I had a good opportunity of directing the attention of the Lyons members of that Jury to my discoveries in dyeing and printing this hitherto intractable silk tinctorially, also in weaving it into various articles of commercial importance, principally plush."*

As well as his display, Thomas contributed an appendix on 'The Wild Silks of India' to the official handbook for the British-Indian Section of the Exhibition, which had been written by Sir George Birdwood. He was also invited to write a chapter on the same subject for a French book, 'L'Art de la Soie', which was published in connection with the Exhibition. This he did, his contribution being thirty-eight pages long, and in French. A further good piece of publicity for Wardles was the greatly admired silk display by Liberty's, for it had been printed at the Hencroft works.

Sir Philip Cunliffe-Owen, who was Secretary to the British committee, spent three months in Paris for the Exhibition. He remarked later that he had dined out every night for three months, *"a feat only possible because I am teetotal"*. Thomas may not have been in Paris for the whole three months, but long enough to achieve the publicity for tussur which he been seeking. *"The President of the Jury told me that it was destined to have an important development in Lyons."* Certainly the Lyons silk manufacturers thought so, as they asked Thomas to put on a similar display at their Musée de la Bourse after the Paris exhibition was over. The original Gold Medal exhibit was put in the South Kensington Museum on its return to this country, while the Government of India supplied the necessary materials for the display at Lyons. It was known as the Wardle Collection and remained on show there for a long time. Four years later, Thomas took some more samples of tussur to Lyons as a supplement to the collection which was still prominently on display, and had a most appreciative letter from the President of the Chamber of Commerce saying how they had treasured the Wardle exhibit ever since the Paris Exhibition.

As a result of the Exhibition, the manufacture of sealcloth was taken up at once by several Yorkshire firms, principally Messrs. Field and Bothill of Huddersfield. For ten years or more it was so much in demand that the manufacturers even bought perfectly good raw tussur and cut it up when they could not buy sufficient waste. Elizabeth had a sealcloth dolman to which Thomas often referred when singing the praises of the fabric: it showed no signs of wear even after several years of constant use, it could be washed and hung up to dry, it was much healthier than a fur as it allowed the perspiration of the wearer to escape, and it did not show marks. Stains could be wiped with a damp cloth, and it did not crease. As for tussur itself, it also became greatly in demand. Despite many exhortations by Thomas, India proved unable to produce the quantities of raw silk required, and the importers had to rely on China to satisfy the demand.

Thomas' triumph was complete when, in the following year, 1879, the French Government made him a Chevalier de la Legion d'Honneur, and an Officier de l'Academie Française, in recognition of his achievements in the silk industry. The exhibition had not only brought him recognition but also very useful contacts. It was through his French acquaintances that he was able to find a weaver for William Morris, and through the same sources he was able to place one of his boys (probably Gilbert) in a French dyeworks where he learned a great deal.

Thomas had not forgotten his research into the dyes and tans of India, as commissioned by Lord Salisbury. He had little time to give when work was pressing, but on his return from Paris he resolved to complete his task. In 1880, he sent the first instalment of his findings to the Science and Art Department of the South Kensington Museum; the second instalment arrived two years later. The Blue Book, as it was called, consisted of eighty-two pages of written material, thirty sheets of woven silk, cotton, wool and tussur, three hundred and sixty sheets in all, with three thousand five hundred dyed samples from one hundred and eighty-one varieties of Indian dyestuffs. For a year, nothing happened, despite enquiries from India as to when it was going to be published. The India Office wrote to the Science and Art Department about it, and finally had a reply from them nine months later saying the Stationery Office would print it if the India Office would agree to take fifteen hundred copies. Consent was given, but while these lengthy

Le Présidens de la République Française,

suiv la proposition du Présidens du Conseil,

Ministre des Affaires Etrangères,

Décrète :

Art: 1er. Sont nommés dans l'Ordre National de la Légion d'honneur :

Officier :

M. Henry Thompson, Exposant britannique à l'Exposition universele 1878.

Chevaliers :

M. John Vills ———— idem ————, grand prix d'horticulture ;

M. Wardle (Thomas) — idem —, grand prix pour les soies ;

Art: 2. Le Président du Conseil, ministre des affaires Etrangères, et le Grand Chancelier de l'ordre sont chargés, chacun en ce qui le concerne, de l'exécution du présent Décret.

Fait à Paris, le 29 mai 1880.

Jules Grévy

c. s. C. de Freycinet

Pour ampliation :

Le Directeur du Protocole,

J. Millard

Decree naming Thomas Wardle as a Chevalier de la Legion d'Honneur
and an Officier de l'Academie Français

negotiations had been taking place, Thomas had been doing more research and had started to send a supplemental report in instalments, *"...I am doing it free so the report will be complete"*. The Science and Art Department wrote again to the India Office, in great annoyance: Mr Wardle now wished to add fresh information, had recently sent a sixth instalment which almost doubled the text, and was unwilling to let it be printed in the original form. After three months further discussion, it was decided to send the report to the Government of India. Arthur Godley, the Under Secretary of State for India, wrote: *"I must say this seems a most judicious although somewhat inglorious proposal. This office has had to recognise from the first that Mr Wardle is an impractical enthusiast and often a very perverse one, as when he insisted on drawing all the botanical illustrations himself in his book on Wild Silk, with the moths in aesthetic contortions instead of scientifically. The long delay in the publication of the present report has, I am told, really arisen from his irrepressible desire to add to it by improvement on improvement and now he virtually refuses flatly to be responsible for it unless he is permitted to perfect it – i.e. in practical terms to almost double it, and probably still further delay the date of its publication.... The Government of India will probably at once publish the report as it stands"*. It did, in 1885, but omitted to send Thomas himself or the India Office a copy, which caused even more general annoyance.

Thomas was disappointed and disillusioned. He complained that even in Calcutta there had been insufficient copies to meet the demand, and that it should have been illustrated in colour. He had barely received his expenses even though he had devoted so much valuable time to it from his business. Through delays, incompleteness and parsimonious printing, *"...my book, as far as any usefulness it possesses either to Europe or to India, is a dead letter and it had been more economical never to have published it"*. Later, Godley did admit in an internal India Office memo that Thomas had been badly treated not to have received an official acknowledgement of his work from the Government of India, but *"no blame to this office in the matter"*. This was the first, but no means the last, occasion when Thomas and Mr Godley had a disagreement.

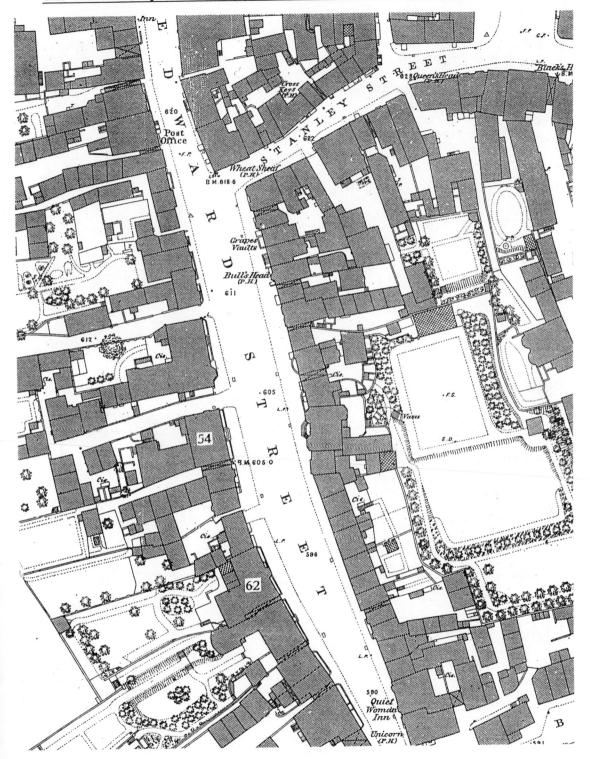

St. EDWARD STREET, LEEK, from the 1879 ORDNANCE SURVEY MAP
Showing the two Wardle houses, No.62 and No.54

St Edward Street, Leek

St Edward Street, Leek

These two old postcard views of St Edward Street show the area as the Wardles would have known it.

Chapter Three

THE WARDLE-MORRIS CONNECTION

William Morris, poet, designer and socialist, was one of the most outstanding personalities of the second half of the last century. He came into contact with the Wardles through his work in fabric design. A very close professional association sprang up between them in 1875 which continued for six years, while their personal friendship lasted until Morris's death in 1896. The first experiments that Morris made in fabric design were for the furnishings of the Red House at Bexley Heath, where he lived in the early days of his marriage. His daughter May said in later years: *"My father would have nothing in his house that was not beautiful and useful. All he could find in shops were a few Persian rugs and some blue and white Delft pottery, so he decided to design himself."* For the curtains, he designed flowers to be embroidered on lengths of blue dyed serge. From these he went on to produce decorative hangings and wall panels, in the softest shades he could find, on coarse plain materials. He disliked the sharp but fugitive aniline colours used in the textile world at that time, and made up his mind to revive the use of the old vegetable dyes. The aniline dyes were only half as expensive and the chemical process by which they were obtained was much quicker and easier, so organic dyes had long ago been abandoned. Morris, with his new ideas on naturalistic design, wanted only to produce articles of simple beauty and did not care if they cost more as long as they conformed to his own standards of quality and beauty.

Not everyone admired his new style in furnishing. Some of his contemporaries considered it strange and unhomely. But he nevertheless went on to found his first business in 1861, called Morris, Marshall, Faulkner and Co. Partners in the enterprise included many names later to be famous in artistic circles: Burne-Jones (with whom Morris had been friendly since they were at Oxford together), Philip Webb, Ford Madox Brown and Rossetti (the only one of them to be an established artist already). The firm's working capital was a loan of £100 from Morris's mother, and it set out to be a cooperative of working artists producing their own original designs.

The new firm managed to keep afloat in the beginning by their commissions for stained glass and wall hangings. Then their embroideries, carpets and patterned textiles began to attract public interest and business began to expand. It was not long before Morris decided to take on a business manager so that he himself could concentrate on the creative side of the work. The first manager died of consumption in 1870, but he had been in post long enough to prove how invaluable it had been to have someone to look after the business side of things if the firm was to continue to thrive.

The next manager was George Y.Wardle, brother of Elizabeth and brother-in-law of Thomas. George was a draughtsman by profession. His first contact with Morris had been a commission to provide drawings of mediaeval designs of tiles, wall paintings and carvings from various country churches. Another order from Morris was for him to put some drawings by Burne-Jones onto wood blocks. George related in later life that he had wondered at the time why no more orders came, as he had been convinced that his second drawings had turned out better than the first. He discovered the reason in the end; Morris, very typically, had decided to try his hand at wood blocks himself.

The commissions resulted in a closer association than George had foreseen, as Morris eventually asked him to join the firm as business manager. George proved to be an able administrator. Morris depended increasingly on his advice, even to the extent of being persuaded to move house to allow the business to develop. For some time Morris and his family had been living at Queen Square in London, under the same roof as the business, but expansion was forcing changes. In a letter Morris wrote "...*we must turn out of this house next Spring, for Wardle wants it all for the business...*"

Other changes were in the air as well. Morris had become increasingly the dominant partner in the firm, and some of his artistic associates had dropped out. Consequently, in 1875, the old firm was closed and a new one registered as Morris and Co. During the difficult and sometimes acrimonious negotiations preceeding this, Morris relied heavily on his manager.

The expanding part of the business was mainly in textiles and embroidery, both fields where Morris found technical difficulties were preventing him from the achievement of his ideal. His pursuit of organic dyestuffs was frustrating. He found dyes for both wool and silk were fugitive: he tried to use only the best, which were mainly peacock blues, rusty reds and olive greens. As soon as he had a small dye house of his own at Queen Square, he struggled to produce permanent colours, experimenting with indigo blue, madder red and yellow. He realised that his own facilities were too limited for anything more than basic trials and to make progress he needed more knowledge and more scope. Within three months of the establishment of the new firm, Morris had been in touch with Thomas Wardle at Leek, probably at the suggestion of George.

For the next two years, Morris spent much time in Leek, having found in Thomas a fellow enthusiast for the revival of the old vegetable dyes. He himself had read widely about past methods of dyeing, while Thomas and one or two of his workmen had some recollections of the old processes they had seen in their youth. But, for both of them, it was a matter of painstaking experimentation. Thomas set aside one of the two dyeshops at the Hencroft works almost exclusively for this work, which was a real mark of his enthusiasm for the project as it reduced his commercial dyeing capacity as a result.

The association between the two men was mutually beneficial, though not always smooth. They were both in their early forties, both with separate businesses and heavy commitments, both at the peak of innovatory energy. Morris gained technical knowledge, found a printer for his fabric designs and acquired some commercial experience which must have been useful when he opened his factory at Merton Abbey in 1881. Thomas, on the other hand, also benefited from the research into natural dyes for his embroidery silks and wools. Many of his patterns showed a strong Morris influence, and it must have been good for the Wardle firm to be associated with a personality as well known as Morris.

After Morris began his visits to Leek in 1875, a correspondence commenced between him and Thomas Wardle, the Morris side of which has fortunately been preserved. In addition, several of Morris's letters home from Leek are quoted in his biography by J.W.Mackail.

The first visit was a success. Morris spent his time with Thomas and some of his men working in the dyehouse, and wrote home that his hands became *"habitually and unwashably blue"*, in no condition to do fine work. The elusive indigo dye was his primary objective. On his return home, he sent Thomas a copy of Pliny, having gone back that far in his research into old methods of dyeing. He was soon back in Leek and wrote to his wife, *"...I can't get back till this day week, I really can't come away till I have seen more results..."* Those first yarns, according to George Wardle, were used for pile carpets and resulted in the first carpet loom being installed at Queen Square. That November, Morris sent a list to Thomas of all the colours he wanted, two blues, a blue–green, two greens, two yellows, one brown and a possible black, *"...with these I can carry out any design I want that does not need madder colours, and setting indigo apart. As to the indigo, when we once get it, Prussian blues and greens will be things of the past"*.

The indigo became an obsession. Morris wrote a paper about the delicacy and difficulty of an indigo vat, with details of the necessary preparation and maturescence. The experienced indigo dyer can tell by the smell if fermentation has been reached. If the right moment is passed, the vat is useless. The yarn must be dipped in it evenly and not allowed to touch the air.

One weekend, Thomas took him to Lichfield, but Morris thought it a dull town in a dull landscape. *"I shall be glad to be back in the dyehouse tomorrow...my hand is shaky with journeyman's work for the last few days...it is hard for the body but easy for the mind"*. Back at work again, Morris wrote home: *"I have been dyeing in her (the vat) all the afternoon, and my hands are a woeful spectacle in consequence. She appears to be all that could be wished, but I must say I should like not to look such a beast, and not to feel as if I wanted pegs to keep my fingers one from the other. I lost my temper in the dyehouse for the first time this afternoon; they were very trying, but I wished I hadn't been such a fool; perhaps they will turn me out tomorrow or put me in the blue vat"*. No such retribution seems to have followed, but the effect of the dyeing on his hands did stop his work as an illuminator for the time being.

Another minor upset occurred shortly afterwards when Morris wrote complaining about the price of four Carnation blocks that the Wardle firm had produced for him. He grumbled that if it did not come down, he would not be able to sell the fabric. This must have provoked an angry reply from Thomas, for the next letter to Leek was conciliatory, asking that work should continue and *"not to leave us in the lurch, as I value working with an honourable and sympathetic person like yourself ...If I can't have my dyes perfect I am prepared to give up that side of my business...We are accustomed to insults and to imitators... Let's try woad instead of indigo for blue..."*

The correspondence continued in 1876. In January, Morris was thanking the Wardles warmly for their hospitality, and soon he was promising to design a special rug for Elizabeth's wool work. The following week he wrote: *"I send you two bits of Cretan embroidery for your museum. They are about 150 years old and, being borders of women's petticoats, have been washed to death. The colour of the greener one pleases me very much. Mrs Wardle will find some stitches in them worth looking at."* Morris himself made a careful study of old embroidery techniques especially from the Middle East, sometimes even unpicking them in order to learn exactly how they had been stitched.

The cooperation between the two men had increased to the extent that, by mid-1876, the Wardle works were dyeing Morris's embroidery silks, carpet wools, silk and cotton yarns as well as printing his textile designs. The first Morris chintz printed by Thomas Wardle was Tulip in 1875, handblocked, printed in madder dyes. Two other early designs were Marigold and Carnation, soon to be followed by Acanthus, Honeysuckle, Indian Diaper and African Marigold. Most of the designs were printed on cotton or linen, but some were produced on velvet, velveteen and silk.

Morris experimented with his dyeing at Queen Square when he was not in Leek. He told Mrs Burne-Jones in a letter that in the course of his own experiments, he had discovered and tried out the ancient craft of weld dyeing, the oldest and fastest of yellow dyes. Poplar twigs also produced a yellow that pleased him. But whenever he could spare the time he returned to the vat at the Hencroft works in Leek. In early Summer he was there partly to supervise the cotton printing and partly to continue his search for the best vegetable dyes. Describing this visit in a letter, he wrote: *"My days are crowded with work, even working in sabots and blouse in the dyehouse myself. You know I like that, and am there pretty much all day long; I am dyeing yellows and reds; the yellows are very easy to get, and so are a lot of shades of salmon and flesh-colour and buff and orange; my chief difficulty is in getting a deep blood red, but I hope to succeed before I come away; I have not got the proper indigo vat for wool, but I can dye blues in the cotton vat and get lovely greens with that and the bright yellow that weld gives. This*

Marigold

Carnation

Acanthus

Honeysuckle

African Marigold

Indian Diaper

MORRIS DESIGNS, BLOCK-PRINTED BY WARDLE

morning I assisted at the dyeing of 20 lbs. of silk (for our damask) in the blue vat; it was very exciting, as the thing is quite unused now, and we ran a good chance of ruining the silk. There were four dyers and Mr Wardle at work, and myself as dyers' mate; the men were encouraged with beer and to it they went, and pretty it was to see the silk coming green out of the vat and gradually turning blue; we succeeded very well as far as we can tell at present; the oldest of the workmen, an old fellow of seventy, remembers silk being dyed so, long ago. The vat, you must know, is a formidable-looking thing, 9 feet deep and about 6 feet square, and is sunk into the earth right up to the top. Tomorrow I am going to Nottingham to see wool dyed in the woad vat, as it is called. On Friday Mr Wardle is going to dye 80 lbs. more silk for us, and I am going to dye about 20 lbs. of wool in madder for my deep red. With all this I shall be very glad indeed to be home again, as you may well imagine."

By August, trouble started again. Morris complained that an unsatisfactory standard of dyeing was creeping in, due to a lack of supervision on the spot. Thomas, who had just turned down a lucrative contract with someone else out of loyalty to Morris, found this too much. He replied that the mental, physical and financial pressure was too great and he was considering giving up the second dye-house. Morris replied with his usual response, that he was unable to let standards slip and must have nothing but the best. He nevertheless hoped that Mr Wardle would continue.

The breach was soon healed: *"I hope we shall go on smoother in future".* And very soon after, Morris was writing to Thomas: *"By the way, shall we dispense with the ceremony of Mistering one another in future, if you don't think me rude?"* He had designed a window especially for the Wardles, perhaps as a peace offering. Commenting, he said he was glad they liked it and they were heartily welcome to it. And more carpet designs were promised for Elizabeth. (The window remained at the house in St.Edward Street until the 1950s, when it was bought by Sir Geoffrey Mander and installed at Whitwick Manor, in the old billiard room.)

Indigo still concerned them both that winter, the alternative of woad having been rejected. The letters came from London to Leek with news of further experiments and suggestions, also, inevitably, some complaints from Morris the perfectionist: *"...the floss and sewings I left behind at Leek have come back un-dyed. I send it back and should be glad to have it dyed as I am rather torn in pieces by my embroideresses."* And again, *"I am disappointed with the honeysuckle, the blotch is too light. Try the spoiled African Marigold dipped in the blue vat since it is our only chance of using it... The madders are none of them blue enough, the carpet is too scarlet..."*

Nevertheless, in spite of dissatisfaction over such matters, the personal friendship between the two men seemed to blossom. They shared a love for fishing, and Morris invited Thomas that summer to join himself and two friends on a fishing and boating excursion near Oxford. All of them thoroughly enjoyed the expedition, and Morris accepted an invitation to call at Leek on his return from a visit to Ireland in the Autumn, to tackle the local grayling. Thomas was to take Morris's fly-rod to be mended locally so that it would be ready for him when he arrived.

A very personal touch came in a letter about this time: *"...My respects to Master 10 when he comes, he will certainly be like a young bear with all his troubles ahead if he has to learn blue-dyeing, but how if it be MISS 10, though?"* The Wardle family was on the increase yet again, and the newcomer turned out to be Elizabeth's last child, a daughter called after herself, another Elizabeth.

During his visits to Staffordshire this year, Thomas took Morris to Alton Towers *("a gimcrack castle of Pugin's")*, to Ellastone and Norbury (where he admired the chancel) and up the Dove valley to Ashbourne. Quite apart from the value of his visits for the overseeing of the work and gaining more experience about dyeing at first hand, Morris seems to have enjoyed himself staying with the Wardles. His letters certainly sound most warm and sincere when thanking them for making him so comfortable.

By 1877, Morris began to wish he could do his fabric printing himself, but without suitable premises he could not undertake that. He was constantly designing new patterns for the chintzes and silks and decided he must concentrate on developing the weaving aspect of the work. In March, he wrote to Thomas saying he wanted now to tackle brocades on his own premises, and asking him to recommend an experienced silk weaver from France. This was not very difficult, given Thomas's close connections with the silk manufacturers of Lyons. Morris was prepared to offer the man 3000 francs a year, but wanted to see specimens of his work before settling a contract. *"I hope your correspondent understands that we want a really intelligent man; if he turns out to be such, his position with us will be good, as we should surely be wanting more looms, and he would be foreman over the others. As soon as we are agreed, he must let us know when he can come and send us some proper paper for pointing, in order that we may get a design ready for him without delay. So much for the brocader, when I have thanked you again very much for getting me on so far, and confessed that I am prodigiously excited about him."*

As a result of the Wardle negotiations, a Monsieur Bazin duly arrived on the afternoon of 25th June 1877. George Wardle was sent to meet him. According to Mr Guy, secretary to the firm of Morris and Co., Morris *"did not feel as if he wished to face Froggy at first but said to George Wardle that he would be up in his room if wanted"*. George, however, was not anxious to exercise his French alone for any longer and took the newly arrived Monsieur straight up to Morris' room where he left him.

Morris had enquired earlier from Thomas what space and height would be required for the loom and its weaver *"....we should by all means want it big enough to weave the widest cloth that can be done WELL without steam power; it ought to be such as could weave a design 27 inches wide (Nicholson can only do us a 9 inch design), this width is what we have hitherto had from Lyons. We should certainly want to weave damask".* But in spite of these enquiries and the proposed preparation of the pointing paper in advance of Bazin's arrival, actual weaving did not start for three months. A Jacquard loom was erected in Ormond Yard nearby and the silk was dyed by Wardle and Co. To begin with, Morris had had to prepare the pointing paper himself, until he had trained other staff to do so. Once the weaving started, it appeared that the pattern was not coming out right, because the cards had not been put in correctly. It is not clear if this was the fault of Bazin but Morris finally had to take on an extra man to help, one who had previously worked at Spitalfields. Eventually the intricacies of the Jacquard loom were understood and many fabrics woven on it.

As well as his new project with the loom, Morris was much occupied with carpets. (Thomas was asked to dye and supply 200 lbs. a week of low quality wool for some three ply carpets which were being made in Yorkshire). He was also trying to vary his fabric designs. They had all previously been derived from flower forms, but he wrote to Thomas that he was spending much time studying birds with a view to incorporating them into his next patterns. In fact, four out of his next six designs did include birds.

In 1878, fourteen textile patterns were printed at the Wardle works for Morris. In addition to the early ones, favourites such as Snakeshead, Iris, Bluebell, Pomegranate, Peony and Little Chintz appeared and became extremely popular. Although Morris had decided that he would have to find new premises and print the textiles himself, the work continued to be done in Leek for the time being, but no new design was introduced for the next few years.

The early Morris designs can be seen in the Wardle pattern books in the Whitworth Art Gallery, University of Manchester, together with fabric samples. The typical Morris repeating pattern was a mirror turn-over style. The whole width of the material was used, 36 inches for linen and cotton, and 24 inches for velvet and velveteen. There is a strong resemblance between Thomas's own patterns and those he printed for Morris. Both men were influenced by Indian and Middle Eastern art, and determined to educate public taste into an appreciation of flowing natural designs. In this, they were successful; Morris's designs became the rage, and even today many versions of them are still popular. He had many imitators once his reputation and popularity were established, Thomas Wardle being one of the many, but at least a very skilled one. This may have been an irritation to Morris, but it does not appear to have contributed to the final break in their business arrangements. Morris's dissatisfaction had been mounting for some time and by 1881 it reached its limits. Samples of bad dyeing were being returned by clients and the printing was taking too long. He wrote furiously to his wife: *"Tom Wardle is a heap of trouble to us. Nothing will he do right and he does*

Snakeshead

Iris

Bluebell

Little Chintz

Tulip

Larkspur

MORRIS DESIGNS, BLOCK-PRINTED BY WARDLE

write the longest winded letters containing lies of various kinds.......we shall have to take the chintzes ourselves before long and are now really looking for premises."

The prerequisites for suitable premises were natural light, plenty of space and a soft water supply. These he found later that year at Merton Abbey, an eighteenth century mill on the River Wandle near Wimbledon, with plenty of buildings for looms, dyeing and workshops. George Wardle supervised the move to Merton but it took nearly two years before the hand-blocked printing was in full production by Morris's own staff and new designs were again registered.

Morris was a hasty tempered man, but he was probably justified in his complaints that the dyeing and printing done for him at Leek were of variable quality owing to inadequate supervision. The last years of the 1870's and the early 1880's were extremely busy for Thomas. His experiments with Tusser silk were taking most of his energy and attention; the Paris Universal Exhibition of 1878, his invention of sealcloth, the development of his embroidery silks and the exhibition of Indian silks at the South Kensington Museum all belong to these years, taking him away from home for prolonged periods. It was not surprising that he was not able to pay as much attention to the work commissioned by Morris as he had done in the earlier years.

The end of the correspondence between the two men dealt largely with the subject of tapestry weaving. Evidently Thomas had suggested a joint venture in this field, but Morris was not encouraging: "the tapestry is a bright dream but it must wait until I get my carpets going", he wrote towards the end of 1877. During the following year, he studied late mediaeval tapestry design and technique, set up a high warp loom and actually started to weave 'Acanthus and Vine' in May 1879. He rose early in the morning to work on it and completed it by mid-September after more than 500 hours at the loom. Thomas had returned to the subject, wanting to manufacture small verdure (foliage) pieces as part of a joint enterprise. Morris put him off with various excuses: it would not be viable financially; it needed a specialist colourist for the figure work; only a good artist could successfully translate a painter's design into the medium of coloured wools on a warp. It was a project Morris wished to do on his own, with apprentices trained by himself. Thomas did not press the matter further, but he demonstrated his admiration for the tapestries when the Morris works began to produce them after the move to Merton Abbey by ordering two for himself. In 1887 two panels were woven for the Wardle home, one of St. Cecilia and one of St. Agnes, adapted from cartoons of Burne-Jones's stained glass work. These panels were exhibited at the Manchester Centenary Exhibition, and both were re-woven the following year, a sure sign of success. Years later, after the death of Morris, Thomas made an unsuccessful bid to purchase two of the three Holy Grail tapestries that had been commissioned for Compton Hall, Wolverhampton, when the owner moved to a smaller house and had to dispose of them. They were finally bought by public subscription for the Birmingham Museum and Art

Gallery.

After the move to Merton, Morris's interest in dyeing waned. He had succeeded in reintroducing vegetable dyes and conquered the dreaded indigo, and his enthusiasms moved on to the high warp tapestries, the carpets and the Kelmscott Press. By now, George Y. Wardle had become more than a business associate. As Morris became more and more involved in active Socialism, so he depended more on George to run the business for him, regarding him as a personal friend. Before making his first public speech to the Trades Guild of Learning, Morris took George along to the hall beforehand and read 'Robinson Crusoe' to him, to test if his voice carried sufficiently. By 1884, George was earning £1200 a year, nearly as much as Morris himself was drawing. When George Y. Wardle retired in 1890, his successors, the Messrs. Smith, continued to run Morris and Co. with similar loyalty and adherence to the same high standards of quality and design.

Although there was little or no business between the firms of William Morris and Thomas Wardle after 1882–3, there were occasions when the two men met, and their personal friendship was perhaps all the stronger once the sources of irritation were gone. The final letter in the correspondence came in 1896, preserved no doubt because of its poignancy. The Wardles had acquired a country 'weekend' house at Swainsley, in the Manifold valley. Delighted with his new acquisition, Thomas wrote to his old friend a glowing account of the unspoilt beauties of the countryside around it and urging him to come and stay there with them. Knowing he was ill, Thomas said he was sure the rest and change in peaceful surroundings would do him good. But it was too late; his reply in August read: *"My dear Wardle, It is very kind of you to invite me to share in your Paradise and I am absolutely delighted to find another beautiful place which is still in its untouched loveliness. I should certainly have accepted your invitation, but I am quite unable to do so, for at present I cannot walk over the threshold, being so weak. The Manifold is the same river, is it not, which you carried me across on your back; which situation tickled us so much that owing to inextinguishable laughter you very nearly dropped me in. What pleasant old times those were. With all good wishes and renewed thanks, I am, Yours truly, William Morris."* The letter had been written in another hand, and ended with a very shaky signature. Six weeks later, William Morris died.

William Morris in 1877, just after the years of his visits to Leek.

No. 54 St Edward Street - second home of the Wardle family - as it is today. Behind the tree is the smaller house, that was used as the shop and work studio.

Mrs Elizabeth Wardle

Chapter Four

LEEK EMBROIDERY

The Society

"Nothing better could happen to young women than to be kept fully occupied, and I hope that the excellent service rendered by Mrs Wardle will extend to other classes of society..." This was Sir Philip Cunliffe-Owen from the South Kensington Museum speaking in 1881 in Leek at the annual prize giving of the art classes. Over a hundred years later it seems strange that this was a sentiment very generally held.

Victorian women both young and old did a great deal of embroidery. They discussed it, compared notes, read magazine articles about it and loved to see exhibitions of it. Older ladies with plenty of servants enjoyed their crewel work, making gifts for their families and for charity bazaars. Wives of self-made men who had prospered in industry did their needlework for the tasteful embellishment of their homes. As for the girls, they had little choice, for their mothers, like Sir Philip Cunliffe-Owen, considered embroidery to be a ladylike and suitable way of spending their spare time.

Since the 1830s, for forty years or so, Berlin Woolwork had been the rage among the ladies. This was a wool on canvas embroidery which had originated in Germany. Usually it was worked from a paper pattern onto a blank canvas, but sometimes the design was printed onto the background. The stitches used were simple, mostly tent, cross and gobelin. It had the attraction that the embroideress needed no particular skill or flair for design; she had only to count the squares on the canvas with accuracy to achieve an effective piece of work. It was the precursor of the kits sold today erroneously described as 'tapestry'. A large range of other forms of embroidery were also in use in Victorian days: appliqué, patchwork, braidwork, beadwork and varieties of white work, to mention but a few, but Berlin woolwork was the most popular form of spare time embroidery for upper and middle class ladies in the mid-nineteenth century.

A change of taste started when William Morris began to influence the artistic scene. His experimental wall hangings, with simple floral designs worked in worsteds on plain serge cloth, have already been mentioned. They were not universally greeted with enthusiasm. One critic wrote that middle class people did not use hangings on their walls and were not likely to furnish their rooms with such homely materials. But others watched the development of his ideas and liked them. A release from the restrictions of Berlin work was at hand, and the 'Art Needlework' movement had arrived.

The would-be Art needlewoman abandoned her canvas in favour of linen, silk and wool. It also meant that if she was to model her work on the new style, she needed practical help and advice on stitchcraft, materials and a supply of suitable designs. In answer to these needs, the Royal School of Art Needlework was founded in 1872. Its foundation was closely followed by the Ladies' Work Society in 1875 and the Decorative Needlework Society in 1880. Where London led, the provinces followed. Branches of similar societies and needlework bodies opened all over the country, including the Macclesfield Embroidery School, founded by J. O. Nicholson M P, and the Leek Embroidery Society, founded by Elizabeth Wardle, to quote two neighbouring examples. When Thomas asked Elizabeth to devise a new form of Art needlework in order to promote the use of tussur silk, it was very well timed, just when all needlewomen were experimenting with new styles and techniques throughout the country.

A printed panel by Thomas Wardle, used for embroidery,
showing the influence of Willam Morris designs.

The exact date when the Leek Society started is difficult to pinpoint; some sources say 1879, most references point to 1880. Perhaps both are true, and it came into being during the Winter of 1879-80. Certainly it was already in existence by June 1880. Its establishment does not seem to have been marked by public acclaim, but maybe that was not very surprising Elizabeth Wardle and a circle of friends had worked on large scale church needlework for 12 years or more, and were well known in the district for the excellence and originality of their embroidery. The transition after Elizabeth's restoration to good health from a group providing church furnishings to a society devoted to the development of art needlework must have seemed a natural progression.

By the time Sir Philip Cunliffe-Owen made his remark about the useful employment of young ladies in November 1881, the Leek Embroidery Society was able to put on a sizeable exhibition of its work. The display contained 18 pieces of church embroidery 'worked by the Leek Embroidery Society and other ladies in Leek and its neighbourhood from the year 1868, superintended by Mrs Wardle': altar frontals, pulpit cloths, sanctuary mats and almsbags. This was the work for which they first became known locally but what was new were 15 items of silk embroidery, described in the catalogue as 'pieces worked with Indian wild silk, Tussur on Tussur; ie. floss of Tussur silk worked on Native Indian woven Tussur silk in Indian design, the colouring by Mrs Wardle and worked by the Leek Embroidery Society and other ladies. The items consisted of a mantel border, a pocket-handkerchief bag, 7 chair backs, 3 curtain borders, 3 unfinished pieces and some studies in Oriental designs which were sewn by 7 ladies, including Elizabeth herself and her sister-in-law, Phoebe. To supplement the local exhibits, Morris and Co had sent 8 pieces of work from their shop in Oxford Street, and the Royal School of Art Needlework had contributed no fewer than 43 items. The Leek Society must have taken pride in seeing its work shown side by side with the London examples. The display of needlework at an art school annual event is interesting in itself as it must signify the acceptance of the new style as an art form in its own right, not just as a ladies' hobby.

Since Sir Philip Cunliffe-Owen was a personal friend of the Wardles, the invitation to give away the prizes presumably originated with them. But even making allowances for the polite comments expected from a personal acquaintance of the family, he does seem to have been genuinely impressed by the work of the new Embroidery Society, and by Elizabeth's skill as coordinator and colourist. A few days later he wrote to Thomas with great enthusiasm:

"...Considering the remarkable success which has attended the Leek School of Art Embroidery it has proved itself worthy of being permanently established as an institution. Mrs Wardle has shown powers of organisation in the interest she has communicated to other ladies in the very beautiful and artistic work she has produced. Now all this depends on Mrs Wardle, indeed her aids, who have shown their love and ability in the work, would be at a loss to fill her place. To found the Leek School of Art Embroidery, to provide a suitable home for it, to have a foundation for the maintenance of the same, including the payment of a mistress, would be a great and good work. It would enable classes of females to attend schools of an evening; it would afford them the example of never having an idle moment, and further would help to revive the great silk trade, and one branch of it, embroidery, which would respond to the growing taste for the same amongst all classes of society. I do not despair that you will find some noble-hearted citizen who will come forward with £5000 to found as a permanent establishment that which under Mrs Wardle's active and organizing mind would become a model throughout the country. From Leek would go out teachers for the numerous schools of art needlework and embroidery which would spring up throughout the United Kingdom..."

The noble-hearted citizen was not forthcoming, but the embroidery school thrived. One phrase in Sir Philip's letter made a point very dear to Thomas's heart; that the new tussur embroidery could help to revive the silk industry. Elizabeth had always been supportive to Thomas in his work, and when he finally succeeded in bleaching, reeling and dyeing tussur satisfactorily, they both saw that her skill as a needlewoman could be useful in promoting it.

51

Having experimented with the tussur floss, she found it eminently suitable for her purpose. The floss was dyed with the vegetable dyes that Thomas had worked with WIlliam Morris to perfect. The soft, glowing colours and lustrous finish were ideal for Art Embroidery, so she devised a unique method of using it, which certainly did bring tussur to the notice of the public.

Leek Embroidery, par excellence, was worked in tussur floss on a printed tussur ground. The printed pattern on the silk substituted for a transfer; when the work was complete the original printed pattern was covered by the embroidery This had the double advantage of providing a guide for the embroideress and at the same time helping to make known the Wardle silks block-printed at the Hencroft works. Thomas' insistence on good design could serve a double purpose: beautiful fabrics would lead to well designed embroidery.

The stitches used were simple: long and short, stem, buttonhole, back and French knots. Couched gold thread from either China or Japan was used lavishly to heighten the effect. Naturally, background was required, when a motif could be appliquéed onto it. Although the ladies' magazines praised the new Leek work because it was so easy to work on a printed fabric and so dispense with the tedious business of transferring the pattern onto its background, yet there was a method for printing designs when required. To quote from 'The Ladies' Field' of 1898: 'One of Lady Wardle's daughters has a cosy little studio, reached by a winding fllght of stairs and overlooking the tennis court at the back of the house. Here, with a most ingenious apparatus recalling a familiar instrument of torture in a dentist's operating room, she traces the designs and by the aid of this contrivance punches tiny holes following every line on the pattern. The actual design is then stencilled in tiny dots on the fabric, where it shows clearly, and it is not liable to be rubbed out by handling'. The daughter mentioned was probably Lydia, the eldest.

Thomas had always insisted that one of the main reasons for the decline of the British silk industry was the poverty of design. From the very first, Leek Embroidery used only the best. The list of the pieces shown at their first exhibition in 1881 contains many adapted from Indian patterns. Even before he visited that country, Thomas had a great admiration for Indian design. (His seven year work on the Dyes and Tans of India meant that he was well acquainted with it.) Lotus scrolls and diaper patterns were effectively and easily adapted to the lines of the Art Embroidery movement. Moreover, the recent imports of Oriental fabrics by Liberty's had given a big boost to the popularity of Eastern designs. The selection of those patterns for the first products of the Leek Society was well chosen.

When Thomas returned from Bengal in 1886, he brought back more Oriental inspiration, the most famous of which was the Ajanta design. This was taken from 2000 year old wall paintings in the Ajanta caves near Bombay. When adapted for embroidery, it was worked on a cream tussur background in lapis lazuli blue, terra-cotta and moss green, liberally highlighted with gold thread.

In his quest for good design, Thomas copied ideas from Persian, Coptic and Celtic art. He visited Haddon Hall to copy the green and crimson velvet curtains of the State bed. All these he used in his fabric printing, but naturally they were available also to Elizabeth for her Leek Embroidery. There were many modern designs drawn for the Leek Society by contemporary artists, such as Walter Crane, Norman Shaw, Gerald Horsley, John Ridley, John Sedding and William Morris himself. Two members of the family contributed designs as well; George Young Wardle, and Tom Wardle Junior. Some of the smaller domestic items were probably designed by Elizabeth herself, with assistance from one or two of the most experienced members of the Society.

The colouring was a particularly pleasing aspect of Leek Embroidery. The vegetable dyed floss came in a vast range of glowing colours, but the skill of using and blending them was all Elizabeth's. With a natural flair for colour, she had impeccable taste, whether she was choosing shades for a teacosy or an altar frontal. No harsh colours were ever used, nor any sharp contrasts. Long and short stitch heightened or darkened the shading almost imperceptibly.

In a Grangerised copy of Sleigh's History of the Ancient Parish of Leek, there is a printed card or label, 3 inches by 1 inch which reads 'Leek Embroidery Society, Branch of the Royal School of Needlework, South Kensington. Mrs T Wardle, Superintendent'. It has not been possible to trace the connection between the two bodies as the Royal School lost their records for this period during the last war, and the Leek records are also incomplete.

To begin with, the members of the Society worked in their own homes, but as the demand for their work increased, a small property next to the Wardle home was acquired. This was the shop where the patterns and materials could be bought, also the workplace where commissions were executed and where classes took place. According to an article in 'The Queen', the Leek Society existed 'for the encouragement of embroidery and the development of it as an art for ladies whose time was not money to them and who did not expect to gain a livelihood by it'. Another contemporary comment was that the Leek Society was not promoted as a commercial enterprise but purely to instruct ladies and girls in the art of embroidery. Nevertheless, in spite of these protestations, that the Leek ladies laboured for the sake of their art alone, they did actually have some professional embroideresses working for them. The scale of their pay depended on a reasonable profit being made on the sale of the needlework. One we know by name was a Miss Bishop, cousin to Thomas. She became Mrs Hunt on her marriage and helped Elizabeth a greatly in the early days. She was widowed and left in great financial need, whereupon she became one of the Society's paid embroideresses. We know that Elizabeth held evening classes for the maids of some of her friends, and these girls became outworkers when they married. At the height of the Society's popularity it is doubtful if all the orders could have been fulfilled without the assistance of these girls. In the Nicholson Institute there is a photograph of Elizabeth surrounded by eleven of her pupils in 1888. They were Leek girls, all looking very young in mob caps and muslin aprons, but there is no record of whether they paid for their lessons. Several of them later became members of the Society. An interesting light on the subject of fees is shed by a letter, also in the Nicholson Institute, from Sir Phillip Cunliffe-Owen to Elizabeth, making arrangements for her to take a resident pupil, the terms being £3.0.0 per week for board and tuition, or £75 for six months.

A multitude of domestic items were produced, some complete and for sale, while others were offered as kits for ladies to work themselves: cushion covers, chair-backs, pocket-handkerchief bags, blotters, tea cosies, fire screens, tablecloths and mats, napkins, dessert mats, runners, bookmarks,

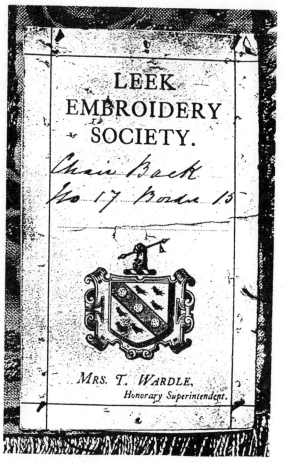

Work label of the type usually attached to the work of the Leek Embroidery Society

borders for photograph frames, piano scarves, and embroidered pictures. Most of them were worked on plain or printed tussur, but other materials were used when appropriate, such as damask or brocade (both dyed by the Wardle works), silk plush, velvet, velveteen and challis (a fine woollen cloth). As finishing touches, lovely tussur fringes were added, or handmade lace with a touch of embroidery.

From an article in 'The Queen' in 1885 it is clear that a mail order system was operating: 'Any lady writing to the Society under the name of Mrs Wardle, Leek, will receive a small parcel containing samples of the embroidery and all information about the price of the materials and the charges for work done'. It is impossible to say how many needlewomen were producing Leek Embroidery, the known names of embroideresses and pupils of the Society number about 50, but there were presumably hundreds of amateur needlewomen who bought the kits and did their own tussur embroidery.

The new style that Elizabeth had created as a means of publicising her husband's silk had become more popular than had seemed possible from its small and localised beginnings. She must have smiled when the Liberty catalogue for 1894 featured 'cotton lengths printed in a single colour outline pattern to be followed by the home embroideress, with specially dyed art silks, all after the style of the Leek Embroidery Society'.

In 1902, Elizabeth died. For 22 years she had organised the work of the Society, devising, adapting and above all, colouring. The needlewomen of Leek had lost the leader who had been their inspiration by her unflagging enthusiasm and skill – things were never the same afterwards. The Society seems to have dwindled away as the demand for the work waned. After being fashionable for so long, it was not surprising that Leek Embroidery went out of favour. Many of the small domestic items had gone out of use, ladies changed their taste in needlework and had less time for it anyway.

The Church Embroideries

The Victorians were enthusiastic church-goers. More churches were either built or renovated in the second half of the nineteenth century than ever before. In the Lichfield Diocese alone, 153 new churches were built in the 24 years between the 1840s and 1860s. And in Leek for the same period, there were four new churches, two Anglican, one Catholic and one Congregational, while the original old Parish Church of St. Edward's underwent a major alteration in the 1860s.

Various reasons were responsible for such an upsurge. First and foremost, there was a genuine religious feeling throughout the country. Then there was the fact that where industrial development had accounted for a large increase in population, earlier provision for worship was no longer adequate. Finally, the Catholic Emancipation Act of 1829 had started a spate of new Catholic churches. All this was good news for the various embroidery societies, for wherever there was a new church or a major alteration there was a call for new furnishings.

It became fashionable for a family to pay for some improvement as a memorial to a deceased relative. Interest in church architecture and the new artistic tastes were widespread. Undoubtedly some churches had not been properly maintained for centuries and were badly in need of repair. People regarded their parish church as a symbol of their community and took a pride in it. Parishioners were more than willing to pay for improvements.

An early inspiration for the architects was Pugin (1812-1852). From him sprang new ideas on church furnishings as well as architecture. He believed strongly that every detail of the decoration and furniture was a part of the whole. The principles on which he based his work were simplicity, good design and good craftsmanship. Although Pugin was among the earliest of Victorian ecclesiastical architects, and perhaps the best known, there were plenty of others to carry on in the same tradition; G E Street, John Sedding, the Scotts, father and son, Gerald Horsley and Norman Shaw. They also believed that every detail was contributory to the whole, and designed all the new furnishings for the churches they either built or restored. The secular decorated arts were reflected in the ecclesiastical work. Windows and embroideries in particular were influenced by William Morris and Edward Burne-Jones.

In 1841 a magazine was published called 'The Ecclesiologist', for the specific purpose of promoting Gothic ideas on architecture and furnishings. Five years later Pugin brought out his 'Glossary of Ecclesiastical Ornament'. The Gothic or mediaeval designs called for new skills, and to help the ladies, numerous societies were formed. One of the earliest was 'The Ladies' Ecclesiastical Embroidery Society', established in 1855 by Miss Street (sister of G. E. Street, the architect) and Miss Agnes Blancome, who used to draw copies of flowers and other motifs used in mediaeval embroideries, so that they could be adapted for church furnishings. Not surprisingly, G. E. Street was a regular designer for his sister's society, and so also was G. F. Bodley. The earliest work done to the new designs was executed in wool on canvas, but when Art Needlework started, different techniques and materials were used. Appliqué work in the style of stained glass windows was often used, sometimes padded or painted, followed by silk embroidery. At the second Great International Exhibition in 1862, all the influential church furnishers were represented. Vestments, hangings and banners showed new techniques, some very elaborate, which were an inspiration to needlewomen throughout the country.

A couple of years later, G. E. Street spoke to a meeting in Durham on the subject of mediaeval embroidery, *"with a view to inspire some of my fairer listeners to emulate these glories of a past age, and to give up the miserable drudgery of cross-stitch, crochet, and the like, in favour of work which admits of delicacy, refinement and art in its execution"*.

Leek was not slow to follow the wave of enthusiasm for church restoration and embellishment. Even a small place like Cheddleton had great changes made to its old church by G. G. Scott junior in 1863/4. The fact that it was at that time the place of worship of the Wardle family must have some bearing on the remarkably distinguished features that can still be seen there; as well as Scott's work, there are windows by William Morris, Burne-Jones and Ford Madox Brown, and a triptych by Morris, Marshall, Faulkner and Company. When the church was reopened, there was much praise for the needlework 'which was executed by the ladies of the neighbourhood'. Much admired were the four alms bags given and worked by Mrs Elizabeth Wardle, also the sedilia cushions given and worked by George Wardle's three daughters, together with two other ladies. Those four alms bags are the earliest known instances of Elizabeth's skill as an embroideress. The Leek Times hailed the new work for its beauty and technique - 'never before have we seen such needlework in this part of the world'.

At Meerbrook, Norman Shaw undertook a large scale reconstruction of the chancel, nave and central tower in 1873, commissioned in memory of the Condlyffe family. To the public subscription, Elizabeth gave one guinea, even though she was not a parishioner, and was to be heavily involved with the embroidery work. She headed the list of the embroideresses, and at the reopening celebrations a special toast was drunk to her 'as the chief genius of the cloths'. A description of these appears in Sleigh's scrapbook; 'a splendid new altar cloth which has been worked in various coloured silks by about 20 ladies, most of them living at Leek, from designs by Mr Norman Shaw under the superintendence of Mrs T. Wardle'.

At the same time, the ladies were busy working a frontal and super for St Luke's Church in Leek, to mark the lengthening of the chancel by John Sedding. Elizabeth involved ten other needlewomen besides herself in this project, including Rose Worthington who appears again later on in this chapter. Ipstones was another instance where Elizabeth led a team of embroideresses to complete a large amount of pieces designed by Gilbert Scott at the time of the church restoration. In 1879 the little church at Millers Dale in Derbyshire was opened. Tiny though it is, it posesses four complete sets of frontals and pulpit hangings in each of the liturgical colours. According to folk memory, they were designed by William Morris. Whether that was so or not, they were worked by Miss Bishop, Thomas' cousin and later a leading light in the Leek Embroidery Society. They must have been made for the opening of the little church or, if not, very soon after. This would make them some of the first church furnishings in which tussur silk was used. After over 100 years, they are still in use and are in excellent condition.

From the time of Elizabeth's recovery and renewed involvement, Leek embroidery was in great demand for church needlework. The tussur silks gave a very wide range of colours, and Elizabeth's eye for colour was one of her greatest gifts. She taught and she arranged work for her pupils, and sometimes she was left with the task of initiating a public appeal to cover the costs of the embroideries requested by indigent customers. She also was often called on to stitch faces on other peoples' work. Fleshwork was a particularly difficult skill. Faces were worked in one strand of silk in one colour only, the contours, shading and features being suggested by the varying directions of the stitches. Two of Elizabeth's daughters mastered this technique, Lydia and Margaret, but there were not many needlewomen who could produce it successfully.

When an arranger was presented with an architect's design for a piece of church embroidery, it was her task to translate the black and white drawing into terms of colour, cloth and stitchcraft. An altar frontal could be anything from 8 to 10 feet in length, and 3 to 4 feet in depth, so it was no easy matter to chart the work for the needlewoman. Frontals were worked on a horizontal frame; in the case of a long one the embroideress could have difficulty reaching the centre of the work. Many of the designs were elaborately embossed. These parts were worked in the hand, usually on fine cotton or linen then cut out and 'glacined'. This was to prevent fraying and to give extra substance to the work. Cotton wool was used for padding if required and the work could then be appliquéed onto the background and gold thread couched along the outline to heighten the effect.

A great variety of materials and stitches was needed to do justice to the very different designs produced by the architects. On the one hand, there would be a Gothic-inspired frontal such as the green 'Four Kings' by Norman Shaw, Leek, with its sombre figures and Gothic lettering, while on the other, the Cheddleton white frontal entitled 'The Three Marys', designed by Gerald Horsley in memory of Thomas' sister Phoebe, is light, delicate and very pre-Raphaelite in inspiration. Threads varied in texture to achieve different effects. Another person who designed church needlework was the Wardle's youngest son, Tom. There is a purple altar frontal and super still in use at All Saints', Leek, which he designed, 'Thou art a place to hide me'. In the same church there is a white set of chasuble, maniple and stole of his design, worked by his sister Margaret (Lady Gaunt).

By 1880, the Leek Embroidery Society was formed in order, according to two of Elizabeth's daughters, *"to cope with the orders which flowed in"*. They recorded their completed church pieces on sepia tinted postcard photographs, some of which can be seen at the Nicholson Institute. These had details and costings written on the back. Prospective customers could choose the design for their commissioned work from these, and copies would cost only about half as much as the original had done. A contemporary account put it thus: *'The Leek Embroidery Society is open to commissions. The work is executed chiefly by girls educated under the superintendence of Lady Wardle, and the good taste which rules every item of work is remarkable.'*

The Society seems to have been well aware of the fact that some of their most dramatic needlework was far beyond the means of certain customers, hence their willingness to work duplicates for a reduced price. They also devised a method of 'working up' printed velvet in gold which achieved a richness of effect with but a small amount of needlework, thereby greatly reducing the cost.

Among the churches that asked the Leek Society to make them some furnishings, there are several from abroad; Port Elizabeth and Grahamstown in South Africa, and Zanzibar and Khartoum. To elaborate on the first two; the link between Leek and South Africa was Rose Worthington, who has already been mentioned as helping Elizabeth in the early days of the Embroidery Society. Her family were silk manufacturers and lived near the Wardles in Leek. The families had a close relationship, with Margaret Wardle marrying the Worthington son and Arthur Wardle being apprenticed to the Worthington works when he was learning the trade. Rose married the Rev Augustus Theodore Wirgman in 1874, and went out to South Africa with him. For the first year he taught at St Andrew's College for Boys in

Grahamstown, then he was made rector of St Mary's in Port Elizabeth. He later became an Archdeacon, and remained out there till he died in 1917.

Since there was no source of embroidered frontals or vestments in the Cape Colony in the nineteenth century, it was natural for Rose to write and ask her old friends in Leek for help. Whether they supplied an altar frontal in the early years that Rose spent in Africa is not known, but in March 1895 St.Mary's was burned down by an arsonist, together with all its contents. Services had to be held in the Town Hall while restoration took place. This must have started immediately, as it was only two weeks after the fire that Wirgman's friend and colleague, Canon Mayo, wrote to the secretary of the Leek Embroidery Society asking for a replacement set of frontals to be made for Port Elizabeth. His list of the money allowed by the insurance claim reads:

1 white frontal and super	*amount allowed £30*
1 blue/violet frontal and super	*amount allowed £25*
1 red frontal and super	*amount allowed £20*
1 white frontal only	*amount allowed £10*

Elsewhere the Canon wrote '...*through the infuence of Lady Wardle, the green, white and violet frontals were supplied at cost price of the materials by the Leek Embroidery Society'*. The £20 for the red Whitsuntide frontal was given by a Mrs Flack from London. It would seem that St Mary's managed to re-equip its church furnishings within the sum allowed by the insurance company. (The red Whitsuntide frontal and super are still being used and still look very handsome.)

Having restored the church and re-stocked the altar linen, it must have been a bitter blow when the same arsonist struck again only two years later. Canon Mayo wrote once more to the Leek Embroidery Society, *"I regret to have to tell you that, owing to an outrage having been committed on St Mary's by a fanatic who burnt our altar, we are obliged to ask you to put in hand another violet altar cloth and super. The other was so beautiful and in every way so satisfactory that I trust you will be able to give an exact replica of it. You charged us £25 for the last, but we hardly expect you to do it so cheaply again. I charged the insurance company £28 (£30 cost in England)."* The Leek ladies did as requested, and according to the Easter vestry account for 1897-98, the sum of £35. 4. 0 was paid to the Leek Embroidery Society for the new violet frontal. In 1970 this frontal had to be replaced, having become very worn.

As a matter of interest, the arsonist, a Miss Frances Livingstone Johnstone, aged 40, had also set fire to another church in 1897, and was caught trying to find a fresh point of attack on St Mary's for yet a third time. She was imprisoned and sent to Robben Island in Table Bay, one of the few institutions that existed at that time for the mentally disturbed.

Several churches have now framed their Leek embroidery frontals and mounted them on a wall for display, thus preventing any more deterioration of the fabric by further use. Others have had the main features of the embroidery remounted. Since much of the most elaborate needlework had been appliquéd onto its background, it was quite easy to remove those parts for rebacking. The work loses a lot of its effectiveness when removed from the intended surroundings and sits uneasily against modern materials. But any restoration is preferable to destroying these examples of Leek craftswomanship.

After Elizabeth's death in 1902, the church work continued to be in demand. Lydia and her colleague Mrs Bill carried on the business from the shop in St. Edward Street. Designs were kept for many years and customers went on commissioning church needlework from these old designs until the shop was finally sold in 1937.

A fine example of Leek Embroidery
Reproduced by courtesy of the Rijksmuseum, Amsterdam

The Bayeaux Tapestry

In 1885, Thomas and Elizabeth were in London and visited the South Kensington Museum. They were met by their friend the Director, Sir Philip Cunliffe-Owen, who showed them some 'cartoons' of the famous Bayeux Tapestry, which had been commissioned by the British Government in 1871. These consisted of an actual size photographic representation made by a professional photographer, Mr Dosseter, and then coloured by hand.

The so-called 'tapestry' is not a woven tapestry but an embroidery on homespun bleached linen using coloured worsted wools. The whole work is 230 feet long and 20 inches deep. It tells the story of the Norman invasion of England and the Battle of Hastings in 1066. Intended to justify the Norman action, it could be described as a piece of mediaeval political propaganda. French tradition has it that the Bayeux Tapestry was made by Matilda, wife of William the Conqueror and the ladies of her court. Recent research, however, both by Mr Gibbs-Smith of the Victoria and Albert Museum and also by the French experts who cleaned and repaired the work in 1984, are agreed that it was from the South of England, the product of a team of English embroideresses. It was probably commissioned by Bishop Odo, William's half-brother, as a gift to Matilda. The presentation of events, the form of the Latin and, above all, the skill of the stitchcraft, all point to an English origin. The expert opinion is that it could have been completed in two years by a number of needlewomen working on frames. It consisted of eight strips of linen of varying length, but one or two feet are probably missing from the end. The English are depicted with moustaches, while the Normans are clean shaven with the back of the head shaven almost up to the crown. Fifty seven inscriptions in Latin above or near the main pictures describe the main narrative.

Elizabeth was fascinated by the work. Embroidery on such a scale had been a magnificent enterprise. As an experienced needlewoman, she could well appreciate how remarkable it was. Obviously designed as a secular ornament with a political message, it had nothing to do with the ecclesiastical decorative art of the Middle Ages. It could not have been more different from the delicate Leek embroidery on which Elizabeth had been engaged for so long. Maybe she had a longing to work with wool again; maybe she felt her ladies were becoming too specialised and needed something different; or maybe it was an impulse reaction to seeing an historic work of art. Be that as it may, Elizabeth conceived the idea that she and her friends should make a facsimile of the Bayeux Tapestry so that England should have a copy of its own.

With typical Wardle thoroughness, Thomas and Elizabeth went to France to see the original at Bayeux. On their return 100 pounds of worsted wools were dyed by Thomas with vegetable dyes to match the eight shades used in the original; terracotta, blue-green, sage-green, buff, full blue, dark green, yellow and very dark blue. The cartoons were borrowed from the South Kensington Museum so that they could be traced by one of Elizabeth's helpers, Miss Lizzie Allen, to ensure the accuracy of the copy.

Thirty five ladies undertook the work, including Elizabeth herself, her daughters Edith and Margaret, her sister-in-law Phoebe and her niece Ellinor. Their contributions varied in size, but all must have worked hard and strictly to the design. It said much for Elizabeth's powers of enthusing her fellow needlewomen that they should venture on such a massive project. It also says a lot for her powers of organisation, since the embroideresses did not all come from Leek: five lived in Derbyshire, one in Birmingham, two in Macclesfield and two in London. Another couple of needlewomen who are not listed officially may have worked small pieces, and the whole embroidery was joined together by yet another lady, Mrs Clara Bill. In just over a year the copy was completed, in less time than the original mediaeval team had taken.

The 230 feet embroidery included 626 humans, 190 horses, 35 dogs, 506 other animals, 37 ships, 33 buildings, 37 trees and the 57 Latin inscriptions. The embroideresses also added their signatures under the portions they had worked, and Elizabeth stitched a final note at the end which read: 'This reproduction of the Bayeux Tapestry was worked at Leek in Staffordshire. The drawings were lent by the authorities of the South Kensington Museum. 35 ladies have been engaged on this piece of tapestry and the name of each will be found underneath her work. E. Wardle, Leek, Staffordshire, Whitsuntide 1886. The worsteds were dyed in permanent colours by Thomas Wardle, F.C.S., F.G.S.'

At some point the Leek Embroidery Society was formed into a company. It is not known exactly when, but probably early in 1886 when the facsimile was nearing completion. Considerable expense had been incurred in the making of it; the tracings, the linen and lining material, the wools, the pressing and making up of the work, storage, etc. The implication is that these were borne by the Society members themselves in the expectation of recouping the costs and sharing in the profits from future exhibitions. It must have seemed a wise step to put the finances on a business footing before it was first placed on show. There is a record among the Bayeux Tapestry papers in the Nicholson Institute showing that a dividend was paid to shareholders at Christmas 1887, and that the secretary for the accounts was Miss B.H.Lowe, daughter of one of the embroideresses.

The facsimile was ready for exhibition at the Nicholson Institute in Leek by June 1886. At 1/- a head it was seen by 1207 people. Single season tickets were also available at 2/-, or a family season at 4/-. It proved so popular that the exhibition was extended for two more weeks than intended though the admission charge was then lowered to 3d. Before the end of that year it had been on show in 5 different parts of this country as well as in America. Wherever it went, the embroidery created much interest and was greatly praised.

THE LEEK EMBROIDERY SOCIETY'S
FACSIMILE OF THE BAYEUX TAPESTRY
IN READING MUSEUM...........

Alderman Arthur Hill, former
Mayor of Reading, who bought
the replica as a gift to the town

This reproduction of the Bayeux Tapestry was worked at Leek in Staffordshire.

The drawings were lent by the Authorities of the South Kensington Museum.

35 Ladies have been engaged on this piece of Tapestry: and the name of each will be found underneath her work.

Leek. Staffordshire.
Whitsuntide 1886.

E. Wardle.

The Worsteds were dyed in permanent colours by Thomas Wardle. F.C.S. &c.

From the Reading Handbook of 1892

The panel at the end of the Tapestry
embroidered and signed by Elizabeth Wardle

In Chester it was exhibited for a whole month. The patrons included the Duchess of Westminster and Mrs Yorke of Erddig. A special committee was set up to handle the event which was based on the Grosvenor Museum and had its own notepaper printed with a scene from the Battle of Hastings as a heading. Complimentary tickets were issued to anyone who had subscribed more than 10/- towards the setting up of the exhibition, but ordinary admissions were 2/- on the first day and thereafter 1/-. Thousands of people went to see it, including the Archbishop of Canterbury, which was recorded with much pride. The tours went on; after America the work was shown in Germany and various towns throughout England. The greatest triumph was at the National Workmen's Exhibition in London where it was awarded a Gold Medal in 1893.

The embroidery brought much praise and recognition, but the exhibitions reaped little financial reward. Carriage costs were considerable and there were other expenses such as the bill from Pullars of Perth for cleaning the tapestry after the Workmen's exhibition, which came to £7.10.0.

By 1895, the share-holders were seriously considering whether to sell their masterpiece. There are unsubstantiated theories that it was offered to the Leek Improvement Commissioners for £400; alternatively, that it was offered to Leek town for £200. but it was turned down. Whether either of these stories was true, it is a fact that when the tapestry was exhibited in Reading Town Hall in June 1895, it was described as 'being on loan with the possibility of purchase'. The person responsible for bringing the tapestry to Reading was a past Mayor, Alderman Arthur Hill, brother to the well known philanthropist Octavia Hill. He told the new Mayor that he was anxious to present something of permanent value to the people of Reading to commemorate the time when he himself had been their mayor.

The minutes of the Reading Town Council record his offer; *'If you or the members of the corporate body share with me the view that this work, absolutely unique in its character and historical interest, would be an acquisition of permanent value to our new art college, and the privilege of possessing it should belong to Reading, I offer the Tapestry with its supports and a large number of printed guides, through you to the Corporation, as a gift to the Borough, only stipulating that if in time to come the work shall be found to occupy too much space and it becomes undesirable to retain it, the Tapestry may be returned to me or to my representative'.*

Reading accepted his gift with gratitude, while the Leek Embroidery Society held a meeting to discuss the matter. It is clear from their accounts that the members must have been out of pocket on the enterprise and when Alderman Hill's offer of £300 was made they accepted it. According to her daughter Margaret, Elizabeth was surprised and bitterly disappointed at the decision. *"She never thought we should allow such a treasured possession to be sold and leave Leek."*

Having deducted £51.9.2 for outstanding expenses, the net profit for the Embroidery Society was £248.10.10. This was divided into 110 shares at £2.5.2½ each. The secretary noted in her letter to members that 'to make even money, Mrs. Wardle has instucted me to pay £2. 5. 6 per share. Considering her disappointment, it was a noble gesture for Elizabeth to pay this extra from her own pocket. Those who had worked on the tapestry were paid according to the amount they had done. Ellinor Wardle, for instance, Elizabeth's niece from Leekbrook, had only worked one yard and two inches and was therefore entitled to one and one eighteenth shares, but the secretary's mother, Mrs Lowe, had done a much larger portion which earned her £10. She spent it on a gold brooch from Pidduck's, the Hanley jeweller and had her name engraved on the back, together with the Latin inscription from the section of tapestry she had embroidered 'Hic fecerunt prandium et hic episcopus cibus et potum benedicit'.

When the facsimile had been at Reading for just under a year, Alderman Hill received a Royal summons to take it to Windsor Castle for the Queen to see. The Court circular for May 13th. 1896 recorded that 'Mr Arthur Hill has had the honour of submitting for Her Majesty's inspection a reproduction of the Bayeux Tapestry which he has presented to the town of Reading and which has been worked by 35 ladies, the majority of whom are resident in the neighbourhood of Leek, Staffordshire.' It must have been a great moment for Mr Hill, and also for the members of the Leek Embroidery Society who read about it. It was displayed in St. George's Hall.

The tapestry was first shown on rollers in Reading, then it was nailed up on a wall in the Small Town Hall like a frieze, being slit in places to make it fit in with the roof. There it remained until Lady Gaunt (the Wardles' daughter Margaret) went to see it in 1927. She was shocked to discover it looking dirty, and in such a dark, high position that she had to stand on a table to see it properly. She wrote to the Reading authorities offering to buy it back in memory of her mother if it was not appreciated.

The council was spurred into action: they had the work cleaned and divided into 25 dust proof frames by Heelas of Reading. A ceremony for the reopening was presided over by Fred Wardle in February 1928, and quite a number of tours were arranged after that for the tapestry, including one to South Africa in 1931. Over thirty years later, the work was again cleaned and remounted by Heelas, in preparation for the 900th anniversary of the Battle of Hastings. Several tours later, in 1984, the facsimile was shown again in Leek to mark the 100th anniversary of the Nicholson Institute, the third time the work had returned to its home town since Reading acquired it. The Staffordshire Moorlands Council took a lot of trouble to display it well, having previously redecorated the Art Gallery in preparation. Once again, the scope and the skill of the work created interest and admiration, this time to a new generation of viewers. If Thomas had been there to see it, he would have been justly proud of his achievement in dyeing the wools with his vegetable dyes as there is practically no sign of fading or unequal strength of tone even after so many years. The stitchcraft of Elizabeth and her friends remains remarkably intact despite all the tours and cutting and remounting.

Sadly, the sheer size of the work meant that the museum in Reading could not accommodate it. For years, one panel only could be displayed at once, while the rest of it was stored in a repository on the outskirts of the town. The difficulties of displaying an exhibit 230 feet in length are obvious. Alderman Hill realised that when he made his stipulation to the Corporation when he presented it – ie, that it should be returned to him or his heirs should the day come that Reading did not wish to keep it. But even in the 1920s when it was so neglected, there had been no suggestion that it should be given back.

Reading now has a new museum. At last there is room to display the Leek copy of the Bayeux Tapestry. The embroidery was the first item to be put in place, in a specially constructed eye-level case very similar to that in which the original tapestry is housed in Bayeux itself. Dim lighting and temperature control has been installed and the greatest care taken in joining the embroidery together.

Elizabeth Wardle with some of her pupils, 1888.
Mrs Wardle
Mary Bishop (Hunt), Nellie Lowe, Cissie Redfern. Kitty Price
Mollie Garside (Billing), Queenie Cartwright (Woodhead), Nellie Vigrass, ? Rowley
?(née Redfern), Nellie McDonough, Annie Brunt (Dishley)

One of the original embroideresses of the facsimile of the Bayeux tapestry reproduced her section
of the work, now in the Nicholson Institute.

Details taken from a superfrontal in All Saints Church, Leek.

The 'green' altar frontal, All Saints Church, Leek

Ajanta design, inspired by 2000 year old rock paintings found in the Ajanta Caves near Bombay. Worked by Miss Annie Redfern.

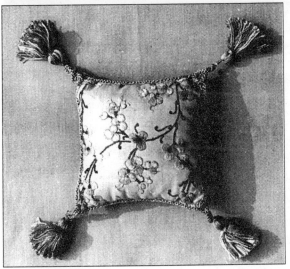

Left: A fine example of the fine and varied work produced by the Embroidery Society.

White Altar Cloth, St Edward's Church, Cheddleton
Three figures appliquéd upon a background of embroidery. Length 7' 3"
Designed by Gerald Horsley

Cross designed by Norman Shaw

White Frontal – Leek Parish Church
The centre figure was designed by John Rigby. The Angels by Gerald Horsley
The Phoenix by Miss Lizzie Allen
This was the last item arranged by Lady Wardle

Two panels from the Bayeux Tapestry

Chapter Five

INDIA AND THE SHOP

For some time Thomas had been considering whether it would be worth while to have a show-place in London where all his various products could be displayed. He was encouraged by the success of Morris and Co., whose showrooms had attracted much attention ever since they opened in 1877. When he eventually decided that a London shop should be his next project, Thomas had to find a reliable partner to manage it, someone who was prepared to spend most of his time in London. The person he chose was his old friend, William Brough, who agreed to manage the shop for three years.

Brough had gone straight from school into his father's business of J. J. Brough, Nicholson and Co, of Leek. At the early age of forty, he was a sufficiently wealthy man to cease active work in the firm and devote himself mainly to collecting works of art. He and Thomas had long been friends, and had worked together well in their Field Club pursuits. Brough had time to give, and his knowledge of fine arts could extend the scope of the shop into ceramics and furniture as well as fabrics. He also probably welcomed the prospect of being based in London for three years near to salerooms and art galleries, where he would have plenty of opportunity to increase his already considerable collection of modern paintings. In 1882, premises at 71 New Bond Street were taken on a thirteen and a half years' lease for a business in Indian Art Drapers, Embroideries and Decorative Furnishers, to be called Wardle and Co. The stocklist for the shop was extensive; there were to be eight departments for silks, velvets, sealcloths, tussurs in many forms including rugs, poplins, woollens, cottons 'with baticks ordered from Leyden', paperhangings, pottery, Delft and De Morgan tiles, furniture and a special department for the Leek Embroidery Society.

At the back of the premises there was living accommodation. The list of furniture purchased for private use does not sound quite so exciting:

Best iron bedstead	Chair for bedroom	Best spring mattress
Rocking chair	Bolster and pillows	Bookshelves
Straw mattress	Pottery	Knives, forks and spoons
Chair for sitting room	Table	

Before the shop opened in 1883, solicitor's advice had to be taken over an agreement between the firms of Joshua Wardle and J.J. Brough, despite the fact that Brough was no longer active in his own family business. The solicitor wrote to Thomas: *"...amalgamation would only be advantageous on certain terms since there must necessarily be a certain antagonism of interest between the two businesses, covering as they do very much the same ground"*. Having decided that matter to mutual satisfaction, Thomas found that he also needed to give an undertaking to Morris and Co. and to Liberty's that he would not undersell them. Both shops sold Wardle products, providing the dye and printing works with much business, and Thomas was anxious to retain their custom. The latter arrangement was to cause much worry later on.

Thomas sent individual letters to prospective clients: *"We aim to put before the public the results of a lengthy experience in true and artistic fabrics for dress and household purposes, avoiding all that is bad and spurious in colour, form and material."* Referring to wild silks, he went on to acknowledge the inspiration given by Sir George Birdwood, "the father of the tussur industry", and the help of Sir Philip Cunliffe-Owen, who as Secretary to the Royal Commission for the Paris exhibition in 1878, took such an interest in the efforts to use wild silks and natural dyes. Not only modern goods were to be sold, but also old work of artistic excellence. *"We shall have associated with us the Leek Embroidery Society, which is now so widely known. The embroidery branch, under the superintendance of a lady of experience, will, we are sure, be a great convenience to our lady customers."*

Brough had enthusiastically drafted an elegant advertisement announcing the opening of the shop. Thomas' comment on it was: *"I like the circular with the exception of the word 'unfading'. I only wish my dyes truly were unfading. I believe this word would bring a loss of confidence as time goes on because it was not a true warranty. I should suggest in lieu ' as permanent as possible'. The word can be used with more safety and truth for embroidery dyes but the best of light on the grounds of plain colours and prints is very severe and in spite of the most careful study I am giving, some colours give way most discouragingly, and I would err on the most modest side of my efforts rather than state what I cannot fulfil."* With this adjustment, the advertisement appeared in 'The Queen' and other leading journals.

The shop unfortunately proved to be a constant source of friction between the two friends. For one thing, Brough made a habit of taking small individual orders to oblige customers, which were not economically viable. Moreover, he was supposed to pay monthly for whatever the shop had ordered from Joshua Wardle and Sons, but he hardly ever did so, nor did he let Thomas have his accounts. With three different works to manage, Thomas had a system of accurate book-keeping and speedy turnover, which was badly disrupted by Brough's unbusinesslike approach.

In July 1883, Thomas was taken very ill. There is no doubt he had been over working, and the subsequent breakdown, or stroke, was the result of years of pressure and strain. (In the records of the India Office there is mention that 'Mr Wardle had been in precarious health for some months and quite unable to persue his chemical investigations'.) Gilbert and his mother took over the correspondence and kept visitors at bay for over a month. He was just beginning to improve, though still in bed, when an incident occurred which was recorded in detail in the Wardle-Brough correspondence now in the Staffordshire County Record Office. Brough had come to Leek, furious over an order for a customer, a Mrs Powell, that had not been executed as required. He went to the Wardle home and burst into Thomas' bedroom in a rage, full of recriminations. Afterwards, although he had hardly started to write his own letters again, Thomas sent a note to Brough saying: *"Both Mrs Wardle and I thought you came into my bedroom in a very hectic state....As I find myself at times very liable to be misunderstood and confess to much clumsiness and want to care in expressing myself, I will ask you as a matter of favour to myself not to take offence from me where none is meant. This matter is lamentably trivial and I confess to much astonishment and a great deal of pain at the time that anything I said - I am sure, pleasantly - could have caused you to return to my sick room with such angry expression and feeling."* A few weeks later, Thomas wrote again: *"I have found that those who are gifted with the power of saying severe things are themselves most touchy of all people when anything is said to them. In this, I often find myself an example and I confess it, hating as I do the tendency in me of want of forebearance."* Whether Brough was mollified by these letters is not recorded, but as soon as Thomas was up and about, trouble flared up again between the two of them.

For one thing, before his illness, Thomas had asked Brough to negotiate agencies in various towns for selling their goods. *"Every mickle makes a muckle"*, he had said, and suggested for a start that Bristol, Brighton, Clifton and Exeter were all places worth investigation. Brough had done nothing about the matter, nor did he ever do so.

But in November, a much more serious cause for disagreement developed. Thomas had started going up to London again, and was disquieted by the quantity of Corah (Bengali) silks that Brough was displaying at the shop, also by the price he was asking for them. On his way to Euston Station, he called at Liberty's in Regent Street and discovered to his chagrin that his suspicions were well founded: Brough was charging less for the Corahs than Liberty's were. When he reached home Thomas wrote to Brough saying that the price must be increased, and it would be desirable not to display them so prominently. Brough resented being told how the silk should be displayed and what he should charge for it, and complained bitterly that he could not do business under 'restricted conditions'. Thomas replied: *"My dear Will, I of course do not wish to overload you with Corahs ... but I cannot see how you are restricted when merely asked not to display too many of them. I have asked you from the first not to under-sell, I have given my word to Morris and to Liberty that we would ask as high a price as they and not in any case lower. I am no price competitor. I have often spoke to you of the folly of underselling. If I had thought you would have ever undersold Liberty, I would have spared you your disappointment by entering on my London project alone. It was an express condition that we should not undersell and it remains an express one as far as I am concerned. I can see success in observing it and ruin to me in breaking it in any respect. Liberty's inform me they are thinking of discontinuing the Corah line, and this after three months ago urging me to double my turning out power. I did so at a great cost, the last new copper vessel being on the way from London this week. Can you wonder at my anxiety? What does Liberty think of my word? I have done my best to assure him that it was an unintentional opposition and that it is rectified, but his disappointment is deep and has ample means of avenging this mistake. If he throws Corahs out of fashion, he hits me so as I have hardly been hit before, for I have spent a large sum in plant and bricks and mortar for this class of dyeing and have six men at work on it. I write without anger or ill-feeling...."*

This was not quite the end of the Corah affair: the next letter asks Brough to observe a request from the manager at Liberty's, Mr Goodyer, that the Corahs should not be so conspicuous outside the shop, but only be displayed inside. The Brough response was a counter complaint that Goodyer was copying his ideas on window dressing. Also, he wrote to Thomas, *"Two shopmen from Liberty's came in after watching Stannard go to lunch, and, finding no-one in but Miss Nowton, priced many articles, turned them over, took down handkerchieves from the shelves and after satisfying themselves, walked away without leaving any names. The special handkerchieves we are selling at 2/6 are from a little lot I bought very cheap, and it has yielded a good profit. They are charging 3/6, but have nothing to complain of. To oblige them, I withdrew them at once. I don't want to make enemies. I want to be left alone to do a business."*

But he could not be left alone, since he was again behind with his accounts. Thomas had asked Brough for a copy of the capital account as he wished to equalise the shares put into the business and was feeling increasingly uncomfortable about it. *"Each letter I get from you, I hope to receive the statement as requested. You asked me to wait for this before sending the money...and now you blame me for not sending it...I not only waited for the promised information but had paid the Watson's overdue account for plush, £300 out of my own pocket, rather than remind you of your promise of the 6th. Don't think I am vexed; contrariwise, I am much amused."*

Since the relationship between the two men was rapidly deteriorating, Thomas felt it necessary to ask his solicitor to write to Brough when the amount owed by the shop to the print works reached £900. In the letter to Brough concerning the persistent non-payment of the printing accounts, the solicitor could only reiterate what Thomas had told his partner so often in the past: *"The print works are separate from No.71 and will only print for customers who settle monthly. Mr Wardle says that, if he is to concentrate on No.71, he must be free from worry about the print works. He has put himself to great inconvenience and loss of business in his printing by giving precedence to small orders for the shop over old and much more valuable customers who pay regularly...His health is another reason why there must be no more trouble with this account. He has a good deal of deficient sleep arising from financial matters and it is very desirable for the sake of his business generally that he has not to worry himself about money matters..."* Brough, who had started by addressing letters *"My dear Tom"*, now wrote, *"My dear Sir, All I get is silly replies from your clerks. I cannot promise you improvement on my part. I must do what I believe to be right and to take my remarks in other than a business sense is to me incomprehensible."*

Brough fell out with Elizabeth too. She wrote to him on behalf of the Leek Embroidery Society: *"I shall not do any business with Wardle and Co. (of Bond Street) unless I can have quarterly payments and a quarterly bill. I shall tell Tom I have received no bill for July although I owe money for tussur cloth. No notice has been taken of my bill, although I am ready to pay all I owe."* Brough replied to her that he did not think he could deal with the embroidery side of the business any longer because of insufficient capital (which was obviously a dig at Thomas), and poor prospects of any increase in trade. He went on, *"...But it might not be wise to deprive us of all examples of embroidery after the paragraph in the circular, though I must do as you wish in the matter. I will not complain about your reporting to Mr. Wardle the nonpresentation of your account, I should have sent it had I known. I should have written to Mr. Wardle but am anxious not to disturb his peace..."*

The correspondence continued through 1884, with increased acerbity. Letters were now addressed "Dear Sir", or even just "Sir", or "Mister". Brough's unbusinesslike attitude infuriated Thomas and certainly caused him great inconvenience, but he had perforce to leave the shop in his partner's hands because of a new undertaking: he was asked by the Royal Commission on Technical Instruction to contribute to its report, on behalf of the silk industry.

This was an honour for Thomas, and provided him with an opportunity to draw the attention of the government to the silk industry. He naturally illustrated his report by quoting details of the Leek manufacturing scene which he knew so well. For the purposes of the report, he studied statistics, and produced many charts and tables to present his facts. Briefly, he reported that three to four thousand workers were then employed in the dyeing side of the Leek industry; thirty handlooms were operating for broad silks, and three hundred power looms; only five or six looms for ferret (narrow tape) were still working; braids and binding, which had once been specialities of Leek, were suffering competition from both Germany and Manchester; buttons were still made in Leek on a small scale, by approximately three hundred people who were paid by piecework earning between four and eight shillings per week; and the most successful product was the sewing silk. He considered that the development of silk in Leek had reached its zenith during the previous decade, the 1870s. He also commented with disapproval on the practice of using sugar to 'weight' the silk, a process which could make a difference of one to three ounces per pound, though it could ruin the fibres if not done carefully.

Regarding the technical instruction required for the industry, his recommendations centred on the need for better art schools and more museums. He was certain that poor design was the major reason why home produced silks were not as popular as the imported Continental ones. *"We have the best climate in the world (for silks), neither too damp nor too dry. Our people are as full-witted as our Continental neighbours, and had their technical and artistic training been as complete as theirs, we should not now be in such as sorry plight."* The teaching given in art schools had no correlation with whatever the local industry was. Only two in the whole country included in their curricula subjects relating to the work in their nearby communities: one was Fenton, which provided design and painting instruction for the ceramic industry, and the other was Birmingham which had courses relating to jewellery. No such provision was to be found in centres of the silk industry such as Coventry, Macclesfield and Bethnal Green, where the local art schools were not influenced in any way by local occupations, and where designers actually had to be imported from France.

Thomas was a great advocate of museums, where the best examples of local craft could be displayed. This would engender a sense of pride in the achievements of a local industry and be a great benefit to the young. *"The next generation will be more educated than this one, we need to provide for its instruction and to give it standards of excellence."* The Report of the Commission was published in March 1875. The contribution made to it by Thomas aroused much interest and was widely praised.

During the gathering of material for his part of the report, Thomas had met many silk manufacturers from different parts of the country, and was very aware of their interest in the Colonial and Indian exhibition due to take place in London the following year. Having played so large a part in the Paris Exhibition, he was naturally hoping that his services would again be required, especially as the Prince of Wales was again to head the Exhibition's Royal Commission, and Sir Philip Cunliffe-Owen would be deeply involved in the event which was to take place at the South Kensington Museum. It may have been partly to keep his name fresh in the mind of the India Office that he sent an unusually prompt reply to a request from them for an analysis of some crushed seed pods of the babul tree. (He found them tinctorially weak, but possessing certain mordant qualities). He also sent to the Under-Secretary of State a copy of 'The Journal of the Society of Arts', for which he had written an eighteen-page article about the cultivation of silk worms. The information came from research done for the Lyons Chamber of Commerce, which resulted in the building of a new silk laboratory there. Every industrial centre in England ought to have a similar research unit, Thomas urged, echoing his recent report. Randolph Churchill, then Under-Secretary at the India Office, was impressed. He signed a memo directing that six copies of this interesting article be sent to the Government of India. *"Mr Wardle is well known for (a) his Dyes and Tans of India, (b) his work on wild silk, and (c) his report on the silk industry to the Royal Commission for Technical Instruction."* Later, Thomas was pleasantly surprised to find that copies of his article had indeed been circulated among Indian silk producers, and had been widely discussed.

Meanwhile, the plans for the exhibition had been proceeding. The Government of India had decided that the largest portion of the Indian section should be devoted to silk. Sericulture in the subcontinent had been greatly on the decline for some years, and it was hoped that by featuring it strongly, the attention of English manufacturers would be redirected to Indian silk. Much to the pride of the Wardle family, it was decided by the Prince that Thomas should be made responsible for assembling the items for the Indian exhibit. This would involve going out to India, and at the same time he was asked to advise the Indian silk producers on how to improve their products so that the very best quality could be displayed in London. Thomas wrote: *"... it was by the mutual consent of the Royal Commission and of the Government of India that I should go out to India, at the sacrifice of much time and personal comfort..."* It was, nevertheless a 'sacrifice' that he accepted with much pleasure, having quite probably suggested it himself. (The India Office in London had not been consulted or involved in the decision to send him to India, and this led to recriminations later on). As his son Gilbert remarked later, Thomas was only able to absent himself from his business because his brother George was there to look after the three Wardle works. Gilbert himself had completed his training and joined his uncle at the Leekbrook dye works, but the next two boys, Arthur and Bernard, had not yet finished their education.

Thomas was due to leave for India in November 1885, and the exhibition was to open the following May. There was much to be done before he left, not the least being another effort to improve the running of the Bond Street shop. Brough had still not paid the printing account; Thomas wrote: *"My not having been paid for my printing for so long makes my overdraft at the bank serious, and troubles me very much. I don't know what comfort is but my life has been a struggle throughout and I don't fear this. It only wants time and patience, courage, tact and determination and all will come right."* He asked Brough to bring his books next time he came to Leek so they could go through them together. As regards the capital account, it still had not been equalised *"... you are too good natured in the matter of credit. I can't put any more in at the moment. I don't wish to disappoint you, but I have had many heavy losses the last two years through bad trade and my Zulu speculation, or I would have equalised the capital investment."* Brough's response was: *"Dear Sir, I am in receipt of your favour which has been perused. I can only say I am much disappointed. I have asked all creditors to pay up in the New Year. If you were better acquainted with the vigilance exercised over these accounts, you would hardly find it necessary to make remarks about my good nature. I have borrowed £900 to pay the printing bill. The plushes are unsatisfactory, I may have to decline to accept them".* (Thomas scrawled in red on this letter: *"I desire to be consulted before any orders are declined".*) Brough deeply resented Thomas' insistence that he should see the books, regarding it as a slur on his honesty. He refused to bring or send them, or to appoint a representative to speak for him as

Thomas suggested. One of the senior employees at the shop heard from Thomas: *"It is much more serious for me than it is for Mr.Brough. He can stand it well, but I can't. But, thank God, I can work yet and must do. I am not going to let it fret me more than it has, nor am I going to be quarrelled with."*

When the capital account was finally obtained from Brough in September 1885, it turned out that Thomas had actually put in £92.2.0 more than his partner, so all the aggravation had been unnecessary. Brough retaliated just before Thomas left for India by saying that more money was needed if the shop was to carry on, and reminded him that the agreement to run the shop had only been for three years, which was due to expire the following April. He declined Thomas' offer to order goods for the shop while in India and said that he did not wish to be involved in any way with the Exhibition when it took place.

Despite his annoyance, with typical impulsive generosity, Thomas went to visit the elder Mr. Brough, and reported that the old gentleman was quite cheerful, and that as long as the doctor went in every day, there seemed to be no immediate cause for alarm. However, Mr Brough senior did die shortly afterwards, which meant that his son was then much involved in clearing up his father's estate and had even less time and interest to spare for 71 New Bond Street.

It was therefore with many misgivings about the shop that Thomas left for India. He went by train to Brindisi, calling on the way to see the latest Italian reeling device, the Tavelette Consomo, at the Paduan Silk Research Institute. He then sailed on the S.S. Ganges on November 23rd, his passage having been booked by Sir Philip Cunliffe-Owen. A free railway pass had been arranged for him, and a small out of pocket allowance of 2000 rupees. On arrival at Calcutta, he fell immediately under the spell of India. To quote his son Gilbert again: *"He revelled in the Indian atmosphere, the manners and the customs of the people charmed him. Everything was so vastly different from the life he had been accustomed to, and the climate did much to give him a new lease of life, for his health and strength at that period had not been of the best."*

Thomas spent nearly a month visiting silk producing areas in various parts of India.

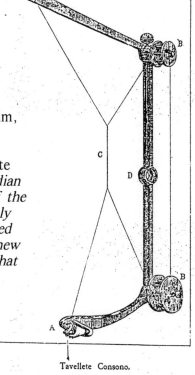

Tavellete Consono.

He concentrated mainly on Bengal and Bihar, as it was the Bengali Government that was to provide the exhibit for South Kensington. But he also went as far as Peshawar, in the North-West Frontier Province, Lahore in the Punjab (where he stayed with John Lockwood Kipling, father of Rudyard) and Poona in the Bombay region. It was en route for the latter that he visited the Ajanta caves and saw the famous rock paintings which inspired the Ajanta design for his fabrics and for Elizabeth's Leek embroidery. The free railway pass was in constant use, and it was remarkable that he managed to cover so much ground in the time available. Everywhere he took notes, gave advice and made new friends.

His two-fold mission had been to collect wild and domestic silk products, from eggs and cocoons to woven fabrics, for the Exhibition, and to examine the cause of the decline of Indian sericulture. He himself added a third: *"to stimulate and give encouragement to an extended production of tussur silk"*. As well as these tasks, he managed to buy quantities of silks for the Bond Street shop, ignoring Brough's lack of interest, and to purchase Indian craft work for his own private collection: brass work, pottery and old embroideries, all of which were later to be much admired by the North Staffordshire Field Club.

A few days at the end of his visit were spent on a shooting expedition. He stayed with friends up country and spent three days on horse back, shooting small local game. Then, as he had an ambition to shoot a tiger, a hunt was arranged for him in the jungle where a tiger was known to have been seen recently. After a two-day tiger drive, with four elephants and forty beaters, Thomas was delighted to find and shoot a Royal Bengal tiger. It was a magnificent specimen, ten feet three inches from nose to tip of tail. The body was taken back to base roped to an elephants back, skinned, and the hide sent to Calcutta to be cured. On arrival at London, it was stuffed and mounted, and was a great source of pride when it finally reached Leek. He made a list of all the animals and birds he shot during his five days of shooting, which makes horrifying reading for the present day reader, but was regarded a hundred years ago as an exciting and praiseworthy achievement. The last stage of his journey back through the jungle to his base was by 'palky' (palanquin) with sixteen men taking turns to carry him through the night. He pronounced it a much more comfortable method of travel than in the howdah of an elephant. Thomas' musical curiosity was aroused by the singing of the men as they jogged through the jungle, reminding him of a Gregorian chant. Afterwards, he asked his host what the words had been, thinking it was some kind of folk song. The words were more mundane than he had expected:

> *"The sahib is a heavy man,*
> *A very, very heavy man".*

On January 8th, Thomas was to make his report on Bengali silk production to a conference in Calcutta. He had worked hard on his notes, comparing all he had seen in his travels of the last month with his previous experience of

Italian and French silk rearing. He had much to say and only an hour or so in which to say it, so he spoke bluntly about the deterioration in quality of Indian silks and the very considerable reduction in the amount produced. He knew at first hand the difficulty experienced in England in obtaining sufficient supplies of silk of acceptable quality from India. Manufacturers now preferred to buy their supplies from Italy or France, silk that was the product of the commercially cultivated Bombyx Mori worm. Bengal silk worms also belong to the mulberry-eating Bombyx family, but are of the 'Fortunatus' or 'Craesi' species. The fibres are almost indistinguishable from those of the Bombyx Mori, but have two features which make the cocoons more difficult to reel: firstly, the cocoon is smaller and therefore more liable to jerk when being wound, and secondly, a greater amount of gum is exuded by the worm round its silken thread. It was in the reeling that the fault lay, Thomas stressed, because there was nothing in the fibre themselves to cause the irregularity of texture which was the chief criticism of Indian silks. He had taken his own pocket microscope to India with him and after careful examination was convinced there was nothing wrong with the Bombyx fibres themselves. The slubs and impurities which made the Indian products compare so unfavourably with the European ones could be cured by better equipment and reeling methods. He strongly recommended the use of the Tavelette Consomo machine, which he had seen in use in Padua at the start of his journey, and described it in detail for the benefit of the silk producers present. The microscope had also revealed that sixty percent of the worms were dying of 'pebrine', a larval disease. Infected eggs were being sold to the growers, who were becoming disheartened by continual bad crops without knowing the reason for them. A scientific research unit could alter all this, by eradicating infected eggs and preventing their distribution.

Disease was not the only reason for the greatly reduced level of silk production in recent years, Thomas told the assembled company. The 'zamindars' (landowners) were to blame for the exorbitant rents they charged for mulberry plantations. This led either to the tenant taking on insufficient mulberry trees to feed his worms properly, or else giving up silk altogether in favour of rice production, for which purpose rents were much cheaper. Another cause of silk worm failure was the hot wind which swept through the matting screens of the huts and killed the worms. He had noticed that in areas where the shelters were built with mud walls, the cocoons seldom failed.

For all these problems, Thomas urged the state of Bengal to take positive action. The disease could best be eradicated by having a silk research institute, similar to those in France or Italy. The landowners could be made to reduce the rent for mulberry plantations. A government forestry officer should be appointed to advise on the care of the trees, in the hope of preventing damage in the future by the prevalent custom of lopping, resulting in many half dead trees and inferior foliage. Finally, the government could give advice on the construction of breeding huts and discourage the use of matting for the walls.

In advocating state intervention, Thomas knew he was making an unpopular suggestion. England, the mother country, always had the policy of leaving industry to private enterprise, and the same attitude prevailed among the government administrators in India. Having seen at first hand the success of active government support for silk production in France and Italy, Thomas could not resist drawing comparisons, unfavourable to England and India alike. Although India, potentially the greatest of all the silk producing countries, was part of the Empire, England was importing seventeen and a half million pounds of silk a year from China, Italy, Japan and France – and only one million pounds from India. Even within India itself, he had seen the silk manufacturers of Poona buying their raw silk from China, and in Lahore silk was imported from Bokhara. All this could change if the Indian producers were given technical help and encouraged to have renewed confidence in their own silk. He had assembled a collection of silks from filatures he had visited, where his improved reeling methods had been used, and assured his audience that the Indian silks could be second to none in beauty and quality.

Lastly, Thomas recommended that the production of wild silks should be developed. He mentioned that he himself had done much to popularise the use of tussur silk. Indeed, after the Paris Exhibition the demand had far exceeded the supply and manufacturers had been forced to buy Chinese tussur which was not such good quality as the Indian, but produced in far greater quantity. He also recommended that special attention be paid to two other wild silks which he had tested and found to be excellent: one was the Eria silk worm of Assam, which feeds on the leaves of the castor oil plant, while the other was the Muga, which eats the leaves of a species of jungle laurel. Both silks were worth wide spread cultivation, said Thomas, and he wished to draw the attention of the government to them.

The silk producers were undoubtedly encouraged by Thomas' assessment of the quality of their goods, and their confidence restored by the prospect of the Exhibition with the opportunity it would offer to show their best silks to the English market. They also took his advice very seriously about eradicating the pebrine disease and wished to invest in the new tavelettes. His report, published in a Blue book after he had gone home, was widely studied.

The government officials, however, were guarded in their response: *"The policy of the Government was to confine any assistance which it offered to private enterprise to the pioneering stage, and that in most directions silk enterprise had past that stage. The Government might do something towards investigating the various kinds of silk worms and moths of the country, and in ascertaining whether the area of useful worms could be extended to other parts of India...There seems no reason why some of the best wild silks should not be more widely cultivated."*

Thomas arrived back in England early in 1886, after an enormous amount of travelling and inspection done in India. He was satisfied that he had been able to give good advice to the Bengali silk producers, and he was happy with the range and quality of exhibits he had managed to assemble for the exhibition. He was convinced that if the Indian silk industry was to develop and reach its full potential, the Government would have to take an active part in rehabilitating it. He had spoken his mind, but he was not very hopeful that his words would alter the official attitude. His doubts proved to be fully justified!

The Bond Street shop today.

Chapter Six

THE ASSOCIATION

On the voyage home, Thomas had written up his notes on his Indian travels. His health was greatly improved; the warm climate, the stimulation of fresh experiences and new friends had acted as a tonic and restored his natural vitality. There was so much to tell his family on his return, and he was looking forward to showing them all his exotic purchases. But the homecoming proved to be very different from his expectations, for during his journey, tragedy had struck. His youngest son, ten-year old Francis, had died. The boy had already been buried in the family vault in Cheddleton churchyard by the time he arrived. The sorrow was all the greater because Elizabeth and the other children had to face it without him.

There was not much time for grief, however, as Thomas had to report to the Royal Commission and start preparations for the exhibition in May, while Elizabeth was deeply involved in the embroidery of the copy of the Bayeux Tapestry. Many years later, their son Fred recalled that every minute of every day seemed to revolve round the family working on the tapestry, for it was a mammoth task. From her own family, Elizabeth had enlisted the help of her sister-in-law Phoebe and her niece Ellinor (George's eldest daughter) from Leekbrook, and two of her own daughters, Margaret and Edith. The other thirty embroideresses did not all live nearby: two worked from London, one from Birmingham and two from Derbyshire. As well as embroidering her own portion, Elizabeth had the task of coordinating the work of them all. Since it had already been arranged that the tapestry was to go on show in June, they had a deadline which had to allow sufficient time for the lining and making up of the two hundred and thirty feet of needlework. Lydia's name was not listed among the embroideresses. Perhaps, being the eldest of the girls, it fell to her to take over the housekeeping and keep an eye on the School so that her mother could give all her time to the Bayeux project.

One of the first things that Thomas did while he was still at home was to call a meeting of the Leek silk manufacturers in the Town Hall at short notice. He was anxious to tell them about his experiences in India, and in particular to impress on them the difference that proper reeling made to Bengali silk. There were 'before' and 'after' specimens to prove the point, together with a small display of the fabrics he had brought back with him. The bulk of his collection for the Colonial and Indian exhibition had not yet arrived, but he hoped that those he did have to hand would encourage the Leek manufacturers to consider buying from India in future. Unfortunately, when the day came, he was ill, and Gilbert had to read his paper for him. Nevertheless, according to the Leek Times, the audience was keenly interested and very favourably impressed.

Leaving his family to their labours, Thomas went to London. He was to be based for the next few months at Norbiton in Surrey, at the offices of the Silk Culture Court. During his absence, the Prince of Wales had decided that Thomas, as Honorary Superintendent, should be asked to write the descriptive catalogue for the Silk Section of the Exhibition. This was logical, since Thomas knew the exhibits and his own reasons for choosing them, but it involved him in a good deal of extra work. With typical thoroughness, he wrote an exhaustive description of the life cycle of the silk worm, with copious illustrations of cocoons, peduncles and even the scales on the wings of a moth. From his travels, he had collected a display of no fewer than fifty-nine varieties of silk-producing lepidoptera, including a wingless one and a tea leaf-eating one. To a public increasingly interested in all forms of natural history, this was to be a revelation, some people previously had only been aware of two or three species of silkworms.

As well as these exhibits, there were mechanical ones: looms and a variety of winding mechanisms. Finally, there was to be a beautiful display of Indian silks and brocades. Also among the exhibits, Thomas made sure to include a Tussur silk 'plush' hearth-rug designed and made for him by William Morris, which was one of his most prized possessions and his best example of the decorative use of Tussur.

All these goods had to be unpacked, listed and assembled at South Kensington by May. Thomas took his second son, Arthur, to London to help him with the last minute preparations. Once the Exhibition had started, he had the use of an office at the museum, and laboratory facilities. The laboratory was necessary as Thomas was required to analyse and report on silk products brought from any of the colonies during the Exhibition. He tested cocoons from nineteen different parts of the Empire during the next months, and of them all he reported most favourably on those from Cyprus. They were very large, and produced very strong silk fibres. These fibres had a larger diameter than any Thomas had ever seen before. Silk of this calibre would be particularly suitable for the manufacture of sewing silks, the speciality of the Leek industry. A ready market could be guaranteed for Cyprus silk if more could be produced. But in spite of his glowing report, it was ten years before Thomas heard anything more about Cypriot sericulture, by which time it was even more in decline than it had been when he had examined it at the Exhibition. As in the case of India, the colonies brought samples to London hoping that the British Government would be convinced of the viability of their traditional silk cultures and could be persuaded to take some active steps towards their rehabilitation. In this, they were all to be disappointed.

In spite of the pressures of the Exhibition, Thomas needed to go home to Leek at regular intervals. For one thing he had a long standing engagement to fulfil in Bradford, to speak to the Society of Dyers and Colourists (he had been their President the previous year.) He collected his usual display of visual aids from Leek and took his third son Bernard with him to operate the magic lantern for the slides. The title of the speech was "Several species of silk fibre and the silk industry". Thomas took the opportunity to talk about Indian spider silk, which was a novelty shown for the first time at the Exhibition. His audience was fascinated by the description of it and the special process necessary for dyeing it. But Thomas went on to say, with great conviction, that the English silk industry was in such decline that *"its extinction was gradual but sure"*. His audience were shocked and critical, but he quoted figures for silk imports and exports to support his assertion. This was not like Thomas' usual incorrigible optimism, and he left the dyers of Bradford uneasy, if not convinced by his arguments.

Another engagement which took him back to Leek was the opening of the exhibition of the completed Bayeux Tapestry in June. It was a proud moment for the family, and a personal triumph for Elizabeth. On the explanatory plaque, Thomas found that his name had been included as well as those of the embroideresses, giving him credit for having dyed the wool for them. He certainly had been very involved in the project, taking Elizabeth to Bayeux to see the original after she had been inspired by the coloured photographs of it in the South Kensington Museum. After her two years of illness, he had been overjoyed to see her well again and keen to tackle a new undertaking of such magnitude.

The main interruption to the business of the Exhibition, however, was William Brough. On Thomas' departure for India, he had left Brough refusing to play any part in the plans for the Exhibition and not wishing to have any new fabrics purchased in India for the shop. Indeed, he had seemed unwilling to prolong his work at 71 New Bond Street after April when his three-year agreement with Thomas was due to expire. On Thomas' return, he found that nothing had been done to increase sales or renew stock, the accounts had still not been completed, but Brough now said he would like to have a stand at the Exhibition. Thomas wrote in exasperation in April: *"...you had previously not wanted anything to do with the Exhibition, now you have changed your mind and I have had to ask Mr Pepper to withdraw in your favour..."*

The stand proved to be the last straw in their relationship. On May 6th, Brough received a letter on official Royal Commission notepaper: *"Sir - Your treatment of me leaves me no option but to decide at once to give you six months notice that I withdraw from partnership with you. I have written to my solicitors to advise me and they will give you a formal notice if they think it necessary. Thomas Wardle."* Brough replied *"...that to act for our mutual interest has been so painful to me throughout this exhibition...your decision is quite agreeable to me."*

As so often with Thomas, his first furious note was followed by a longer, milder letter, in which he said he had told Brough some weeks previously that he would have no time to attend to either his Leek businesses or to the affairs of the Bond Street shop until after the Exhibition was over. Brough had nevertheless plagued him daily with complaints, and had persisted in buying new goods for the stand, refusing to put on sale the silks that

Thomas had brought back from India for the purpose. However, wrote Thomas, *"I have no wish to be unfriendly in any way and shall do my best to consider that your painful and unprovoked attack was due rather to want of control than ill-feeling."* If the letter was sincerely intended to be conciliatory it failed in its purpose. There was still a sting in it and Brough seemed to be even further aggravated. He continued to refuse to release the books of the business or to discuss the accounts. However, it was agreed that the business should be wound up at Christmas and the premises let or the lease sold.

The quarrel between the two old friends cast a cloud over the last part of the Exhibition and for many months to come. There were problems about taking into stock the Indian silks left over from the Exhibition, and many cross letters about the accounts. Mr Donner, Brough's chief assistant, who had helped at the shop since it opened and was also at the Exhibition helping on the stall, requested that he be allowed to buy some of the stock when the clearance sale was held in November 1886. Thomas was quite agreeable to this: *"...he has served us well..."* The result of the sale, however, upset him very much. In a most uncharacteristically shaky hand, he wrote that it was wretched and should have fetched at least £1000. The shop lingered on a much reduced scale after Brough and his share of the goods had gone until the partnership was legally dissolved in 1888. It did not prove easy to sell the lease, nor to sell off the new printed silks, so Thomas suffered a considerable loss. However, an agency was arranged at Debenham and Freebody's to sell the products of the Leek School of Embroidery, which actually proved more satisfactory than the shop had done. And Wardle dyed and printed materials continued to be sold by Morris and Co., and also by Liberty's, so London outlets still remained despite the failure of the shop. Had Thomas the time to give it more of his personal attention, the story might have been very different.

Brough and Donner decided to take a stand at the Glasgow Industrial Exhibition during the Winter months, 1886–87, in order to sell their share of the stock of 71 New Bond Street. Between them they had goods worth about £650. Brough went home to Leek, and paid Donner £5 per week to look after the stand. In the Stafford Record Office are the almost daily letters written by Donner in Glasgow to Brough in Leek. Nothing seems to have gone right. He complained that the electric light did not work and they had to rely on gas; the refreshment room caught fire on the opening night; and in spite of the presence of the Mayor and other dignitaries at the opening, the subsequent visitors were a poverty stricken lot. *"The show has a bad name. Everyone has lost money at this horrid show, several of the exhibitors are broke and are sloping around to avoid payment on their stands..."* Donner grumbled constantly that he was unwell, disappointed and miserable. Moreover, he considered the Scots were a mean, ignorant lot and he was sorry he had ever seen them. Donner finally sent for his wife to join him. On her journey to Glasgow on the train, she reported that Thomas had been a fellow passenger though he had not recognised her. The Donners were much mortified that Thomas did not leave the train at Glasgow in order to visit the exhibition, but travelled further north instead. The daily laments from Donner did not endear him to Brough, nor persuade him to improve on the £5 a week even though the presence of Mrs Donner had increased her husband's living expenses. At the end of the exhibition, Donner had only managed to sell £149.7.3 worth of their goods. Brough was furious, while Donner continued to grumble about the damage to his health caused by the cold and snow of Glasgow, and seemed unmoved by the disastrous financial result of the enterprise. Finally, the last £500 worth of goods were sold by auction in Edinburgh in May, to the considerable loss of both men. This was the last business venture for Brough, who concentrated thereafter on public service, finally becoming a Staffordshire County Councillor and a Guardian of Cheddleton Mental Hospital.

When the South Kensington Exhibition was over, Thomas had more time to follow up his Indian interests. He had received many compliments about the descriptive handbook he had written for the occasion. He was satisfied that the quality of the exhibits had shown Indian silk products to their best advantage. He must also have been pleased that the Journal of Fabrics and Textile Industries published a most complimentary article about him, saying *inter alia* that *"the new tussur silk industry in Europe had been brought about by the indomitable energy and perseverance of Mr Wardle"*.

Self-confidence led him to disregard caution. Being increasingly anxious lest his advice on sericulture was not heeded in India, he wrote several lengthy letters to the India Office, where they were received by Arthur Godley, then Under-Secretary of State for India. Thomas had enclosed correspondence from various silk brokers and manufacturers which showed firstly, that the improved reeling resulting from his advice had led to the sale of all stocks of Bengali raw silk; and, secondly, the great interest in Tussur silk shown at the Exhibition. He asked for the letters to be forwarded to the Government of India for the Viceroy's perusal, together with his own recommendation that official encouragement be given to the production of wild silk. He also sent a copy of the Exhibition's descriptive catalogue, *"a further contribution to my work for India"*, suggesting that it, together with the report of his meeting with the Calcutta silk conference, should take the place of a report of his visit to India. Since no reply was forthcoming, he asked his good friend Sir Philip Cunliffe-Owen to write again, enclosing copies of the same correspondence, to the India Office. Yet another letter from Sir Philip was needed before any action was taken, the second time saying that H.R.H. the Prince of Wales had directed him to express the hope that Thomas' letter, with the accompanying correspondence, might be forwarded through official channels to his Excellency the Viceroy of India.

From the internal memos of the Revenue and States Department of the India Office, Godley's comments amounted to an outburst of fury. He wrote: *"Nothing more is needed to be done, and nothing more SHOULD be done, than to acknowledge Mr Wardle's and the Prince of Wales' letters in the most formal manner. Mr Wardle is a very great friend of mine, partly because I take a lively interest in his work, but chiefly because I cannot help pitying him for the unfortunate way he has in all he undertakes for the good of others, of blundering into his own injury. He is a man with whom it is impossible to have any business transactions, so certain are they to involve you in interminable consequences of the most aggravating and vexatious character. He is a blind enthusiast and particularly is it necessary to avoid giving him the coldest word of encouragement, or he is sure to regard it as a contract of partnership in his work. He had no commission whatever from the Government of India in connection with the silk show at the Exhibition. He went out to India entirely on his own responsibility."* Of course, Godley went on, since Mr Wardle had been entrusted by the Prince of Wales to assemble the silk items for the Exhibition, when he arrived in India he was given official help in his project including a free rail pass and a small allowance for his out-of-pocket expenses. *"To the royal Commission, he was an unmitigated nuisance, for which, however, Sir Philip Cunliffe-Owen's complaisance in dealing with Mr Wardle in the first place, is in some degree responsible. It is obvious that this Office has nothing to do with the copies of correspondence forwarded by Mr Wardle and the Prince of Wales, or with the catalogue of the Silk Court at the Exhibition, and Mr Wardle, being the man he is, it is desirable in order to avoid ever being entangled with them, that the words in which the receipt of his letters are acknowledged should be as few as possible."* As an afterthought, Godley added: *"In my opinion, the correspondence should not even be transmitted to the Government of India."*

Thomas's mission had indeed been arranged by Sir Philip in his capacity as Secretary to the Royal Commission for the Exhibition, with the support of the Prince, and had no official sanction from the India Office. In view of the royal patronage, it had gone ahead, but bureaucratic feathers had been badly ruffled. When Thomas wrote of his *"work in and for India"* and then sought to influence the Indian Government's sericultural policy, Godley's resentment boiled over. He regarded it as an unpardonable intrusion into the province of the India Office for a business entrepreneur to try to influence official policy. The reasons for what Thomas had done during the Exhibition to warrant being described as *"an unmitigated nuisance"* were not specified. It would have fitted the Wardle character, however, for him to have collected far more exhibits than there was room for and then to fight unremittingly for them all to be included. Whatever the facts, the civil servant's attitude and that of the blind enthusiast were diametrically opposed. Nevertheless, Godley did finally bow to the royal wishes and dispatch the offending correspondence to India.

Meanwhile, life in Leek was full of interest and success for the Wardle family. Gilbert had finished his training and was working at Leekbrook under the supervision of his uncle George. The next two sons were still being prepared for their entry into the firm, Arthur in Leek and Bernard spending several months at the German dyeing centre at Crefeld. The Leek Embroidery Society was enjoying much favourable publicity from the facsimile of the

Bayeux Tapestry. After several thousands of people had seen it at Leek, it was then displayed in the gallery of Stoke Town Hall at the loan exhibition put on for the celebration of the 21st anniversary of the North Staffordshire Field Club. As well as the embroidery, the Wardles produced for the display Thomas' very extensive collection of fossils and the stuffed birds that he had shot in India. Thomas must have been gratified to receive a special mention in the President's address for his contributions to the club: *"Mr Wardle, a splendid hybrid, learned alike in geology and palaeontology, who has been our chief instructor in mountain limestone and the fossils therein."*

The following year was Queen Victoria's Golden Jubilee. All over the country special celebrations were planned, and England's Third City, Manchester, decided to have a big exhibition to mark the occasion. In view of his experience, it was not surprising that Thomas was appointed chairman of the Silk Section. The organisers hoped that many of the exhibits from the Colonial and Indian Exhibition could be kept together and displayed again in Manchester. Many of the South Kensington items were indeed shown again, but Thomas was determined that the Silk Section should not merely be a repetition. He said later that much work and research was done during the year which separated the two exhibitions. Certainly this was reflected in the entomological display in the Silk Section. Whereas in London fifty nine silk-producing lepidoptera were shown together with their larvae and cocoons, at Manchester there were two hundred and sixty five varieties.

At Manchester, Thomas was nearer to home and less under pressure from officialdom. Accordingly, he included a good selection of Wardle exhibits: under his own name, there was a display of printed materials from the Hencroft works; Joshua Wardle and Sons had a stand, and so did the Leek Embroidery Society. And this time Thomas took Gilbert with him to help, making him Honorary Secretary to the Silk Section.

The descriptive catalogue was again written by Thomas. It was even more exhaustive this time. It was published in hard back, with two hundred and thirty-eight pages each edged by a golden frame, with eighty-six illustrations. In the introduction, Thomas included several significant comments on the English silk industry. For one thing, if sales were to equal or surpass those from abroad, he urged the manufacturers to take collective action to attract public attention to their wares. *"The industry was in a flourishing state thirty years ago, but the last few years have unhappily witnessed a great decadence. We purchase £11-12,000,000 of manufactured silks from the continent while our own towns have to decrease their output. We must improve our techniques and design so that ladies actually prefer English silk..."* He also suggested a silk journal for the industry, similar to those being published abroad.

The Manchester exhibition gave Thomas a splendid opportunity to meet the English manufacturers. He knew those from nearby Macclesfield and Congleton, but most of the other silk weavers and importers were present from all over the country, either as exhibitors or as viewers. His suggestion that they all needed to cooperate in order to promote English silk fell on receptive ears. Accordingly, before the end of the exhibition, a conference was held in the silk section room to discuss the promotion of the United Kingdom silk industry. The most influential person to take an interest in the matter was Lord Stanley of Preston, later Lord Derby, who was then President of the Board of Trade. He wrote: *"We feel very much at the Board of Trade that we need some central organisation which would make us in touch with the silk industry of this country, for we know very well that our returns are very imperfect; we want instructing a good deal; we have much to tell such an association, and we hope that one of the principal resolutions of this conference in Manchester will be the appointment of a Silk Association".*

The Lord Mayor presided over the meeting, which included a representative from the Board of Trade, specially sent by Lord Stanley. This gentleman drew up a formal resolution, and the Silk Association of Great Britain and Northern Ireland was duly formed in October 1887. This time, Thomas had the cooperation of the civil service and matters were resolved in the conventional manner. The objects of the Association were:

1. To promote and maintain the silk industry of Great Britain and Northern Ireland.
2. To encourage the production of raw silk in India.
3. To collect and disseminate useful information to members.
4. To promote technical, commercial and linguistic education and any necessary Parliamentary legislation, and generally to help expansion in the silk trade.

Thomas was elected Chairman, a position he held for the rest of his life. The conference decided that the members of the Manchester Silk Section should form part of the Council, and then other names were added until the number stood at 69. They included Sir George Birdwood of the India Office, Arthur Nicholson and E.A.Worthington of Leek, and also Gilbert, the youngest of them all. Membership was open to any manufacturer, merchant, dyer, finisher or anyone interested in the silk industry. The minimum subscription was fixed at one guinea. There were to be two meetings a year in Manchester, while the annual meeting and dinner would be in London every June, to coincide with the Silk Sale week. (The first annual meeting was held on June 19th, 1888 at the Cannon Street Hotel at 3pm, followed by a dinner at the Holborn Restaurant at 7pm, for which the tickets cost five shillings.) Some fourteen years later, the Prince of Wales became Patron of the Association.

Thomas was naturally delighted that an Association had been formed. It had long been one of his dreams that everyone connected with English silk should share in its promotion. Frank Debenham was his Vice-President and Lazenby Liberty was on the Council, so he had the support of old friends from

London as well as from the provinces.

One of the first things he did was to send the rather grand 'prospectus' to the India Office asking Lord Cross, the Secretary of State, to sanction a subscription of £5 to the new Association, for which five copies of the as yet non-existent journal would be supplied, four of which were to be for India. Lord Cross agreed, remarking that *"support should be shown, and the information gained could be useful"*. This may not have pleased his Under-Secretary, Arthur Godley, who had recently had another brush with Thomas. This time it was over a new reeling machine which was being tested in Victoria Street. Thomas had written suggesting that the French lady reeler who had been demonstrating at the exhibition should be asked to give her opinion on the new machine. Godley wrote angrily in his internal memo: *"Mr. Wardle has no business to make such a suggestion and I heartily disapprove. He is always confusing things together in this way and creating infinite inconvenience and annoyance to those associated with him. I say this most reluctantly for he has rendered, and is rendering, invaluable service to the silk industry throughout the world. But that is nothing to do with this Office directly, and it should never again allow itself to be led into mixing itself up with Mr. Wardle's labours in connection with the silk industry"*. Lord Cross' support for the new Association must have rankled with his Under-Secretary.

From the time of his return from India, Thomas wrote to the India Office nearly every month. Sometimes it was on a fairly minor matter, such as requesting permission to reproduce illustrations from his 'Handbook of Wild Silks' in another publication, or asking that a small collection of moths with their cocoons and raw silk be sent from India for the Castle Museum in Nottingham. Several times he wrote to report on new reeling machines he had discovered. (One of these was brought over from America after Thomas has corresponded with the American consul in Paris about it). All new developments in the production of wild silk, whether tussur, muga or eria, were described in detail. As Arthur Godley still regarded the silk industry as being of no direct concern of the India Office, these communications tended to be coolly received but were usually, albeit reluctantly, passed on to the Indian Government.

A belated and somewhat heated correspondence arose concerning Thomas' expenses in India. He had overspent his allowance of 2000 rupees by nearly double; in his claim for reimbursement, he unfortunately used both English and Indian currencies, which made the matter very confused. Although it was conceded that the money had been spent on its rightful purpose, also that the allowance had proved to be inadequate, he should nevertheless have sought permission for his spending. Finally, a letter was sent by the ever obliging Sir Philip Cunliffe-Owen to the Viceroy himself: *"The labours of Mr. Wardle are well known to your Excellency's Government in connection with the silk and dyes of India, and it is the opinion of those who are qualified to judge that the commercial results of his work on this occasion will be among the greatest benefits which India will have derived from this Exhibition. Mr. Wardle has been waiting two years for a settlement of his claim. As he has neither received or claimed anything for the time and attention he personally devoted to the success of the India Silk Court, it would be only fair to treat him in a liberal manner and to repay his expenditure".* As a result, it was finally agreed that Thomas ought not to be out of pocket and that his claim for £70.3.4 plus the sterling equivalent of 2015.4.0 rupees be settled at the rate of exchange that had been current at the time of his visit. It had taken two and a half years and much correspondence before this matter was settled.

Despite the battle over his claim, Thomas' greatest concern was to ensure that his sericultural advice to the Indian Government was heeded. With the examples of France and Italy in mind, both of which had silk research institutes, he had repeatedly urged that a similar establishment should be set up in India. Also that someone should be sent to Europe to be trained in microscopic research. The pebrine disease Thomas had diagnosed would not have spread to 60% of the silk worm population if use of a microscope and modern methods of breeding had been understood. He considered that if only one person were sent to learn the necessary skills in Europe, the knowledge could be passed on to others and a proper research centre could be established.

In this latter respect, Thomas' advice was followed. A well-educated young Indian, N.G.Mukerji was chosen, and sent to both the French and the Italian Institutes for short periods of observation. After that, he went to Paris to study under Pasteur, and thence to England to the Agricultural College at Cirencester. Mukerji kept a detailed diary recording all that he had learned, together with his own observations. As they were produced, these notes were sent to Thomas for monitoring. He pronounced himself delighted. The notes were painstaking and thorough, reflecting great credit on the author. One entry in Mukerji's diary must have amused Thomas: *"June 10th 1888. Wrote a paper for Mr. Wardle to read at a silk conference in London, in a railway carriage..."* This was the address to the first annual meeting of the Silk Association, at which Mukerji was the guest speaker.

Thomas wrote an eight page commentary on the young Indian's working diary, *"so long because I was so interested..."* He went on to say that he had been so keen for India to have its own sericultural laboratory that he had even suggested having it at Leek, where he was prepared to do the work for nothing as long as the premises and apparatus could be supplied. But now he felt sure that Mukerji was quite capable of running it himself at Calcutta or wherever was most convenient. His new scientific knowledge provided an ideal opportunity for India to reorganise and encourage her silk industry to meet the European demand. Chinese silk from Canton was getting dearer every month, and Thomas could undertake that the manufacturers of Leek alone could use more raw silk than Bengal was then producing.

With the two exhibitions over and the Silk Association established, Thomas could spend a bit more time on his old pursuits. Both he and William Brough resumed their previous practice of leading expeditions and reading papers for the North Staffordshire Field Club. The legal partnership between them was dissolved in the Autumn of 1888, and after that the relationship seems to have healed despite the extreme bitterness of their dispute over the shop.

Thomas was still friendly with William Morris although they no longer met much on business except for exhibitions. Morris' growing commitment to socialism and to the Kelmscott Press meant that he left more of the fine arts work in the capable hands of George Y. Wardle. However, they did meet at the meetings of the Society for the Protection of Ancient Buildings, and Thomas was still the Society's correspondent for Staffordshire. This had not involved him in very much work over the years, but now a crisis arose: it was proposed to alter St.Edwards Church in Leek, the old Parish Church. The plans for a new chancel had been prepared by G.E.Street, and Thomas was horrified when he saw them. He appealed immediately to the Society for help in opposing them. He wrote offering hospitality to the secretary so that he could see for himself the proposed alterations to the ancient fabric, adding that if any furthur details were needed, his brother-in-law could explain as he knew the church well. The Society did write to the Vicar, but to no avail and the old chancel was replaced by a new one.

George Y. Wardle had been an active member of the Society ever since it started. In 1888, it was decided to send a couple of members out to Venice to report on the deterioration of its ancient buildings, and on the condition of the Duomo of St. Mark's in particular. George and Professor Middleton were the chosen pair. This seems to have come at a difficult period of his marriage, and after his return from Italy, there was a rift with his wife Madeleine. When he retired from the Morris works two years later, he moved out to Fulham on his own.

Madeleine stayed on in Bloomsbury with their two children for a while. Still very much under the Morris influence, young Tom was arrested for speaking at a Socialist meeting. But when she ran out of money, Madeleine arrived in Leek and threw herself on the mercy of Thomas and Elizabeth, her brother- and sister-in-law. Generously, Thomas let her have a small house in Leek, where she caused raised eyebrows by her henna'ed wig and Bohemian clothes. Her habit of laying her china and silver on the table without a table cloth also caused comment. Her husband was remembered by many, since he had been brought up in Leek, but his estranged wife found North Staffordshire society little to her taste, after all her years in London. When she was able, she left Leek, marrying after George's death in 1910 to a man much younger than herself. She outlived her second husband as well, and ended her days in America, dying at the age of ninety-two.

Margaret Elizabeth, the Wardle's second daughter was the first of their children to marry. At the age of twenty, she married Major Philip Jukes

Worthington of the Leek silk manufacturing family. She had known him all her life, and Thomas was delighted. He himself composed and arranged all the music for the marriage service. Margaret's brother Arthur was working at that time in the Worthington factory to gain experience, earning £1.10.0 per week. He must have been pleased when an extra day's wage was paid to all the staff to celebrate the wedding of his sister to Philip Worthington.

To return to the new Silk Association, there were problems of marketing English fabrics. Thomas was convinced that if ladies could be persuaded to abandon their preference for French silk, the decline in the home industry would be arrested. He had always had a gift for public relations, and it was at his suggestion that a special Ladies' Committee of the Association was formed. The object was to spread recognition of the quality of our own silks, and to increase the demand for them. It took nearly two years to gain sufficient support before the new body could be launched, but in 1890 the Ladies' National Silk Association was formed, under the Presidency of H.R.H.The Duchess of Teck. This coincided with the first London exhibition of silks put on by the parent Association at Tatton House, St. James's Square, the town home of Lord Egerton of Tatton. An impressive list of names had been assembled for the Ladies' Committee: 1 Duchess, 3 Marchionesses, 5 Countesses, 3 Ladies and 1 Honourable, with Thomas himself listed as Hon. Working Secretary, Leek. Aristocratic ladies they all were, but Thomas put them to work at once to run the exhibition. The ladies were not only to hang and arrange the exhibits in the ballroom at Tatton House and take care of the stewarding, but also had undertaken to bear any deficit that might be incurred. The main Association had few funds yet, so the ladies received their instructions: "...*in order to avoid unnecessary expense, each lady of the committee has consented to take a day at the exhibition in her turn and to be responsible with her friends for its duties. Owing to the great expense of advertising it has not been possible to make it known except very partially through newspapers and it is left for each lady to invite for her own day.*" Elizabeth and one of the Countesses were to preside over the opening day.

In the programme, Thomas wrote: "*It is hoped by this small exhibition public attention may be attracted to the excellence of English silks. Such an exhibition cannot be regarded as exclusive but merely tentative until the more representative and complete one which is projected and which it is hoped will be held in the Imperial Institute in the Spring of 1892.*" (In the event, this did not take place.)

During the preparations for the show, Thomas had yet another skirmish with Arthur Godley. He wanted to display the latest powered reeling machine, but Lord Egerton would not have it in the house. So, with great temerity, a letter went to the India Office asking if they would pay for a room, as an adjunct to the exhibition, to accommodate the machine and a small gas engine "*of turning power to the extent of one-eighth of a horse – a trifling sum of £50 or so.*" Needless to say, no grant was forthcoming, and the internal memo read: *"Mr. Wardle has done excellent work in connection with the utilisation of Indian silks but he is unfortunately a very unbusinesslike man. If a grant was made, more might be asked for. The costs of the exhibition should be borne by those who will benefit financially by any increase in the silk trade."* So arrangements had to go ahead without the gas-powered machine. But this minor disappointment was quite forgotten when a most gratifying outcome of the Tatton House display was reported in the press:

> *Her Majesty The Queen graciously commanded Mr. Wardle to forward a selection of silks manufactured in this country to Buckingham Palace for inspection. Lady Spencer and Mr. Wardle chose the selection and arranged it in the Palace drawing-room. Her Majesty was accompanied by Princess Beatrice, Princess Christian and Prince Henry of Battenburg. Princess Christian, after viewing the display, remarked: "Well, Mr. Wardle, there is now no more need to go to France for silks, is there?" Her Majesty spent two hours inspecting the silks, kept an assortment and commanded other specimens be sent to Windsor Castle".*

Thomas' pleasure and satisfaction can be imagined.

With the excitement of his daughter's wedding and the affairs of the Silk Association, Thomas was extremely busy, but he constantly had in his mind the question of Indian sericulture. By 1889, he was becoming frustrated and disillusioned. He had put all his knowledge and enthusiasm into his reports and advice, but a short visit was not long enough to achieve a change of attitude towards a declining industry. When Mukerji was sent to Europe to learn modern methods, Thomas felt he was tantalisingly close to effecting the change in Government policy he had hoped for. But as months went by, it became clear that the bulk of his advice was not going to be followed. Mukerji did indeed set up a sericultural laboratory for Bengal at Berhampur, but Thomas had urged repeatedly that what was needed was an Imperial institute rather than a provincial one. He had visions of a silk research centre for the whole of India, even for all the silk producing countries throughout the Empire, similar to those he had come to know and value so highly in Europe. As President of the Silk Association, he could now write with more authority than as an individual. This he did, begging the Government of India on behalf of the Association to form a new department with special responsibility for the silk industry. The Association received a polite reply: their views would doubtless stimulate even further the energetic prosecution of the measures already being adopted by the Government of India and that of Bengal.

Within a few months, it became clear what this 'energetic prosecution' was. The Indian Government announced that it considered the experimental stage was finished. Any further research was to be turned over to a committee of silk merchants, although the services of Mukerji and a small grant of money was to be available for the first year or two. The more elaborate apparatus that had been bought for the research laboratory was not considered necessary and was to be put in the museum in Calcutta. When Thomas heard this, he wrote to everyone he could think of. He went to the House of Commons to see his Member of Parliament, and persuaded Sir Roper Lethbridge to ask a question about it in the House. He wrote of wasted opportunities, of all the work done so far ending in a fiasco: *"...the whole of this important experiment has been handed over to three European firms, which will probably end in an abortive result. Why can't the Government of India recognise the importance of sericulture, at a time when Bengal silk is in greater demand than ever?"*

Predictably, the India Office in London was annoyed. Horace Walpole, and Lord Cross, Secretary of State at that point, both were inclined to agree with Thomas that control of silk matters should not have been handed over to European business men without prior consultation. But Lord Cross agreed with his staff that Thomas' letters would have to be edited in future before they were sent on to the Indian Government. These letters continued unabated: *"...And what will happen when all help is withdrawn? It will probably be said that, as the experiments were successful, the natives can carry on now on their own. Those who know anything about the natives of India will, I think, not expect much persistance or perseverance from them. It is a domestic industry for the peasants, not like tea or indigo."*

Sir George Birdwood was then in London, working as special adviser to the India Office, and even he became wearied by Thomas' constant complaints about the arrangements for the Indian silk industry. Sir George wrote in an internal memo: *"All of Mr Wardle's letters have been forwarded to the Government of India. Several times there was no reply, but when the answer came it was to say that they have carefully considered suggestions made by Mr. Wardle and are satisfied that the necessary experiments are being done properly, and the merchants on the Silk Committee have been most helpful. If the Secretary of State wants to do anything more about it, Mr Wardle should be asked for a paper on it. Personally, I have never understood why he insists so fervently on control by the Imperial Government, as those most affected are Bengal and then the Punjab. Please return memo – I have to write them so often on this subject and want to keep the correspondence dates for reference. I am dead sick of the whole matter."*

Eventually, Sir George was evidently asked to try to stem the flow of letters and to persuade Thomas to moderate the tone of them. To him, Thomas wrote: *"...I am much obliged for your letter and will endeavour to observe its advice in future. I find it very difficult to write these letters correctly, being in the habit of calling a spade a spade, but it is none the less kind of you to correct me...it is very disheartening when one sees so much governmental care in France, Italy and elsewhere, and find our own government will do nothing, or worse than nothing..."*

Nevertheless, no matter how irritating Thomas' protests were to all concerned, it was official policy both here and in India to support the new Silk Association. Information on the latest developments on silk in India was sent out for the benefit of members, while a lecture by Thomas to the Society of Arts on Tussur silk was considered sufficiently important by Lord Cross that he sent twelve copies to the Viceroy with the recommendation that it be translated into the vernacular for distribution in India.

The silk journal that Thomas had envisaged as a mouthpiece for the Silk Association did not materialise. As a compromise, the Leek Times was prevailed upon to publish their accounts, reports of their meetings and the latest information of interest to the silk industry. After a year or two, this role was taken over by the Textile Mercury.

In preparing the industry's reports for the Board of Trade, Thomas was greatly helped by his knowledge of statistics. When he had prepared his report on Technical Education, he had realised how important it was to present figures in an organised manner. He accordingly studied the subject in depth, and in 1887 had been elected a Fellow of the Royal Statistical Society. As with all his interests, he kept up to date with the latest developments in statistics for the rest of his life.

As well as ensuring that the Association kept in regular contact with the Board of Trade, Thomas took up various issues on behalf of the silk industry. One of the earliest problems he was asked to deal with was the cost of freight charges on the railways. The manufacturers complained that the home industry was being crippled by the rates charged for carriage of silken goods. They argued that the system was unfair on two counts: firstly, because 84% of the weight of their freight was in the spools and the packing and only 16% was actually silk; and secondly, the rates for mixtures containing silk were charged the same as for silk itself. Thomas headed a delegation to see the railway manager at Manchester and they did succeed in achieving an amendment to the Carriers' Act.

Another campaign concerned Government contracts for home industry. Thomas had always felt it was wrong for the Government to award foreign contracts for any silken goods needed for the Armed services. The main culprits were the War Office, for powder bags and flags, and the Admiralty for sailors' black neckerchiefs. These neckerchiefs were issued annually to sailors. The cheapest tender had been accepted, for a foreign silk that was so adulterated by chemical weighting that the dye came off on the men's necks and they had all rebelled. Thomas was consulted about it; after analysis, he found that the wefts of the fabric had been weighted by as much as 300%. He instructed the Admiralty chemist in the method of analysing the weighting of silk, and suggested standards that should be insisted upon in future. After that, the dye did not come out any more, the neckerchiefs lasted longer, and – finally – it was English silk, not foreign, that was awarded the next contract.

These were minor triumphs for the new association, but to Thomas the most important objective was to convince the womenfolk of Britain of the excellence of their own silk. The Tatton House exhibition had been small, but had made a impression on public demand, especially after the Queen herself had showed such an interest. Four years afterwards, the Association decided to hold their largest and most prestigious show of English silks, at Stafford House, the London home of the Duke of Sutherland. This splendid house at the head of the Mall, nearest to Buckingham Palace, is now known as Lancaster House. The ballroom provided a magnificent setting for the exhibits.

The out-book of Mr Wright, Secretary to the Duke, has several references to the upheaval caused by the preparations for the event. The caretaker complained furiously that workmen had arrived over a fortnight early, that they had taken rough materials into the house and were actually constructing stands in the State rooms. It had been arranged that the preparations should not begin until a week before the exhibition was due to open, also that all stands and platforms for display were to be made up elsewhere and brought in complete. This must be stopped, said the caretaker. But a letter came from Mr Wright saying that the Duke had consented to the work going on. Not surprisingly, a big loom was to be among the exhibits, and that alone took some considerable time to set up and put in working order. Mr Wright obviously had every sympathy with the caretaker, for he added, *"We cannot have a state room turned into a workshop, they will want careful watching..."* A week later he wrote again to say a detective must be engaged for inside the house as well as the uniformed policeman at the door (to protect the contents of the house, not the exhibits). He ended his letter: *"I hope all your arrangements are going on satisfactorily. How glad you will be when it is all over".*

The exhibition opened on May 8th 1894, and lasted for ten days, from 10am to 6.30pm daily. The entrance fee was 2/6 on Wednesday, and 1/- other days, with the catalogue priced at sixpence. The Duchess of Sutherland wrote the preface to the catalogue. Not only was she the hostess, but also the Hon. County Secretary for Staffordshire for the Ladies' Silk Association. She wrote: *"...it is perfectly possible for England to enter boldly into competition with foreign countries as regards the Silk industry if she receives the patronage and encouragement of her countrymen".* The catalogue listed 67 stands in all, displaying silks, brocades, damasks, brocatelles, velvets, satinettes, failles, veloutines, taffetas, moirés, glacés, grosgrains and silk serges. Some exhibits had been given by the Duchess of Teck, patron of the Ladies' Association. At the back of the catalogue, Lister's advertised their rainproof silk seal and their sewing silks; Courtaulds advertised crêpe *'English crêpes are the best, fashionable in Paris and indispensable for all mourning';* while Debenham and Freebody advertised taffeta glacé, the latest fashion for young ladies' gowns.

A short article by Thomas also appeared in the catalogue, in which he deplored the practice of leading dressmakers still looking to Paris for their materials, although home silks were not dearer than the French and nowadays just as good in design. The membership of the Ladies' Association had risen to 800, but presumably Thomas considered recruitment had been too slow because he went on to urge the Ladies' Committee to obtain 1000 members each, all prepared to ask their dressmakers to supply English material. He added that provincial dressmakers needed more instruction in their art, and praised Staffordshire for being the first County Council to give grants for the teaching of dressmaking: *"an expert from Manchester takes a class in Leek"*.

Some of the crowds attending the exhibition doubtless went chiefly to see the inside of Stafford House. But it was well reported in the press and created a lot of new interest in English silks.

There was one exhibit at Stafford House of which Thomas was more proud than anything else. The notice beside it read: 'R. Mukerji, Director of Sericulture, Srinagar, Kashmir, Small experimental Silk Cloths, manufactured in London from the first raw silk from Kashmir.' It was probably hardly noticed by the general public, but it represented years of effort by Thomas and was a small but tangible proof that his latest dream could come true.

To explain how the Kashmiri silk came to be displayed, it is necessary to go back eight years to Thomas' visit to India prior to the Colonial and Indian Exhibition. While he was out there, he made many new acquaintances, with whom he had kept up by correspondance. Two of these were John Lockwood Kipling (father of Rudyard), with whom Thomas had stayed in Lahore, and Colonel Parry Nisbet, the British resident at Srinegar in Kashmir. Although he had not had time to visit Kashmir, Thomas had heard accounts of its climate, which was not dissimilar to that of Southern Europe, and the fact that mulberries flourished there. The Bombyx mori silk moths were gathered by the natives from the forests, the only place he had ever heard of where they could be found in any number in the wild. Through letters he enquired more about Kashmir from his two friends, becoming increasingly interested in the country. When Colonel Nisbet sent him some raw silk for examination, Thomas was impressed with the quality, even though the price was uncommercial. He began to hope that in Kashmir he might achieve what he had failed to do in Bengal: that is, to establish a flourishing silk producing industry. In the past, silk had been cultivated in Kashmir and had been encouraged by some of the Maharajahs. But, as in Bengal, disease had wiped out the commercial side of the industry. *"Why did the silk fail?"* asked Thomas. *"That is easy to tell. Ignorant procedure. Letting silk-worm diseases have their own way...Ignorance of the scientific work of Pasteur, and of the present methods of prevention of disease, which he alone first formulated...Wherever mulberries will flourish, silk can be profitably produced."*

After a couple of years of informal letters, Thomas felt he was making headway... (The correspondence had a long pause at one point, when Thomas had been away from home, Elizabeth had put his letters on his dressing-table to await his return – one from Colonel Nisbet had fallen down behind the furniture and was not found for six months until Spring cleaning. He had enlisted the support of other acquaintances whom he had met briefly while he was in India. Both Kipling and Nisbet responded with interest to his ideas. They seemed to think that a revival of the silk industry would be possible – the climate was right, the mulberries were there, and there was no shortage of peasants in desperate need of paid work.

The first official letter Thomas wrote on the subject to the Government of India was in 1891, and had to go first to Arthur Godley. Fortunately for Thomas, Sir George Birdwood was still at the India Office, so he wrote to him as well. *"He at once took the matter up very warmly,"* wrote Thomas some years later, *"I indeed owe much to him for the frank, unreserved confidence he always placed in me and my opinions, and several times I discussed the matter with him both by letter and orally; and very great credit is due to him for all he did in furthering my ideas and actions. In short, from the first, and down to the time of his retirement from the India Office, he has spared no pains in giving me every encouragement in my work. He directly conducted the whole of the India Office official correspondence with Kashmir from 1891-1902."* At last Thomas was free from having to act through Arthur Godley and had found a supporter in the India Office.

Almost at once, steps were taken to reorganise the remnants of the old industry, with R. Mukerji as Director of Sericulture for the State. (This was not the Mukerji who had been sent to Europe to study under Pasteur and whose working diaries had won such praise from Thomas.) Although the available equipment was very imperfect, small quantities of silk were produced quite soon. In February 1894, Thomas wrote to Sir George Birdwood that if eight pounds of raw silk arrived in time from Kashmir, he would have it made up into pieces to be displayed at the Stafford House exhibition. *"I have a deep conviction that the future of the silk industry in Kashmir will be of great importance, and that if the Maharajah thinks favourably of the idea, Kashmir may become one of the greatest centres in the world for sericulture"*. The raw silk did arrive in time, and it was made into brocade by Warner and Sons of Spitalfields. It was the first fabric made from Kashmiri silk to be seen in this country. Thomas made a point of showing it to the Queen and to the Prince and Princess of Wales, who apparently evinced much interest. No wonder Thomas was proud of this piece of brocade. It is unlikely that silk would have been revived without his drive and enthusiasm, which was all the more remarkable as he had never been to Kashmir and all his knowledge of the ecology was derived from letters and books.

Chapter Seven

THE 1890s

The 1890s were a time of consolidation and success for the Wardles. Thomas was now in his sixties, prone to bronchitis, had lost much of his hair and was increasingly portly. But there was no diminution of his energy, both physical and mental. His genial and lively manner had made him friends at every turn of his life, none of whom he forgot. The passage of years had made him more irascible, more intolerant of any contradiction, but the harsh words were soon forgotton – by him, if not by the recipients.

The silk industry as a whole, his own three businesses in particular, were ever at the forefront of his activities, but he always found time for his geology and the Field Club as well as his recreations of shooting and fishing. At an age when many industrialists would think of retiring, he was still embarking on new enterprises and interests, while not abandoning the old ones. He was very involved in local affairs, in spite of frequent absences from home; he was one of the Improvement Commissioners for Leek, Chairman of the new Technical Institute, always maintaining an active interest in the work of the Nicholson Institute. He was also Chairman of the Leek Town Lands Trustees, Vice-Chairman of both the cricket and football clubs, President of the Leek Orchestral Society and churchwarden at St. Edward's Church. He even retained an interest in the parish affairs of Cheddleton. Although no longer resident there, he was elected Chairman of the Freeholders' Committee, no paper honour but involved with long and complicated dealings with the Charity Commissioners. Moreover, in 1899, he was elected President of Leek Literary and Mechanics Institute. That same year, he presided at the annual meeting of Leek Memorial Cottage Hospital. With increasingly frequent attendances at court, Thomas was indeed a leader in the affairs of Leek.

The Wardle sons and daughters were very close to their cousins at Leekbrook, sharing many interests. Two of George's daughters were encouraged by Thomas to attend art classes in Leek; Mildred and Ellinor. Ellinor passed with distinction in perspective, and later drew fossils beautifully to illustrate one of her uncle's books. She was one of the few members of the family to join the Field Club, and lent items on several occasions for exhibitions as well as being one of Elizabeth's most experienced embroideresses. There is not so much evidence that the other Leekbrook nieces participated in the same interests, though one or other of them was usually included in the party when the Wardles attended a ball or some other large event in the town. What does not emerge from contemporary records is Thomas' relationship with his younger brother George, who had run the business for so long during his many absences. There is nothing to show whether George preferred to work hard behind the scenes or whether he resented his elder brother's more exciting life. His name never appears at any of the exhibitions or on any committee, he was not even a member of the

Silk Association. But we do know that George got on well wlth Gilbert when the young man joined the Joshua Wardle works. Later when his own son, Horace, also came into the business, there was no conflict between the cousins. Indeed, Horace eventually married his youngest cousin Elizabeth, whose birth had precipitated her mother's serious illness, and who was eight years older than himself.

Undoubtedly the person Thomas was most fond of at Leekbrook was his sister Phoebe. It was she who had taken over the task of playing the organ and training the choir at Cheddleton when Thomas and Elizabeth had gone to live in Leek. She died in 1891 at the age of 51, which was early in such a long-lived family. A Burne-Jones window was placed in the North aisle of Cheddleton church in her memory, depicting St. Cecilia playing an organ.

Of the Wardle sons, Gilbert the eldest was best known in the neighbourhood because of his sporting achievements. As a footballer, he played for the Corinthians and for Leek. He was a member of the Leek team that reached the third round of the English cup in 1885, and two years later was selected as a reserve for England. He also belonged to the cycling club, and was pictured in the Leek Times on a penny-farthing.

Meanwhile, Arthur had finished his apprenticeship at Worthington's and started at the Churnet Works in partnership with his father. There is a photograph of him in the paper as Captain of the Leek Fire Brigade during the hard winter of 1895, when the engine was drawn across Rudyard Lake.

Fred, son number four, had a different career, as a solicitor. His first job was in Bradford, where he was Town Clerk. Later, he set up a practice in Bath. Although he was the only one not to be living in Leek, he kept up with all his old friends there and maintained his interest in his home town and the family business.

Bernard, the third son, had been trained in Germany at the print works of Adophus Meig at Mulhoussen, and took over the Hencroft printing business. He never got on well with his father, but was however a very gifted fabric printer and his youngest brother Tom, worked in partnership with him for some years.

Tom had attended Newcastle High School and then had gone on to study design both at the Manchester School of Art and at South Kensington. In a speech to the Manchester School of Art some years later, Thomas said that it was on the advice of William Morris that he had sent Tom there. Tom's earliest designs were for the borders of his father's pamphlet on craft teaching by Technical Schools, and also for the catalogue cover of the Tatton House silk exhibition. He went on to be the designer-in-chief for the Hencroft Works. His mimosa design was perhaps his best: blossoms in many shades of yellow shading to white, with leaves in many shades of pale green on a self coloured green tussur ground. The Ladies' Field mentioned it with much praise the year it was first produced. He also designed for the Leek Embroidery Society. One example still extant is a stole at All Saints' Church in Leek, designed by him and embroidered by his sister Margaret (by then, Lady Gaunt).

Tom's artistic talents were frequently called upon by the family when they were engaged in one of their favourite pastimes: amateur dramatics. When the Leek society put on 'She Stoops to Conquer', the cast, which included Lydia, Edith, Fred and Arthur, were all dressed by Tom. On another occasion, when the Leek Philothespians chose to perform a German play, which was translated for them by Fred, the set was designed by Tom. They were involved in many an entertainment in aid of charity; both Fred and Tom had good voices and could be persuaded to sing on these occasions. Edith and her cousin Ada from Leekbrook were geisha girls at one very successful fund raising affair. Thomas had a collection of silk banners and flags which were much in demand as decorations for festive occasions. When the Football Club ran a Bal Masque in the Town Hall, Gilbert, Fred and Horace were on the organising committee, and the Wardle flags were used to add colour to the proceedings. A Bal Masque was a novelty for Leek, but unfortunately the masks became so hot and scratchy that most of the two hundred guests had unmasked before midnight. The young Wardles were very active in the social life of the town.

When Bernard and Tom took over the Hencroft works, it was at the height of its reputation. They still printed some materials for Liberty's even though the shop now had its own dye and block printing works at Merton, near to those of William Morris. Several of these Wardle-printed fabrics were shown at the Liberty Centenary Exhibition at the Victoria and Albert Museum, mostly cottons and velveteens. Arthur Liberty was one of those who agreed wholeheartedly with Thomas about the need to improve English fabric design and had set up a new school for it. The late printing done for him at the Hencroft Works were all products of the top designers of the day: Butterfield, Leon Solon and Walter Crane, produced during the early 1890s. Despite the high quality of their work, within ten years the Hencroft Works was in financial difficulties. Thomas had to guarantee an overdraft of £1500 at Parr's Bank for the firm, and lend a substantial sum to each son as well.

The early days of Arthur at the Churnet Works were not auspicious since he started when there was an eight month old dyers strike, affecting Joshua Wardle's as well as the Churnet Works. Wardles had been paying a standard wage of 18/- per week – the men wanted £1, and some of them even talked of one guinea, plus recognition of their union. Thomas had refused, saying he could not afford the increase in wages and that his firm paid as much as any other dye works. Crisis point was reached when union funds were used up, and the strikers had to appeal to the public for help. A deputation of six dyers went to meet Thomas and Arthur at the St.Edward Street office, accompanied by a reporter from the Leek Times which had been invited to send an observer. Gilbert was not present because he was away from home, but the men asserted that he had told them that his father was willing to meet their demands. Thomas had started the meeting with great restraint, but he very abruptly refuted the claim made on his behalf by Gilbert.

The men supported their claim by quoting Hammersley's, (also dyers in Leek), as paying their employees £1 per week, but the Wardles insisted that the standard rate in the two firms were the same and that only those men who were worth more were paid £1. (When questioned by Arthur, it transpired that the man leading the deputation was in fact already earning £1 per week, and was not a member of the union. Nevertheless, he had been elected to speak for the strikers.) Of the 74 men working at Joshua Wardle's, 30-40 remained at work and did not wish to belong to a union anyway, which gave the Wardles a negotiating advantage.

After the chilly start to the meeting, Thomas told the deputation with surprising candour that Arthur had not succeeded in making a profit since he started at the Churnet Works, which were only kept going out of regard for the workers and their families. Arthur could have turned the corner in a few years, but the strike had put paid to that. Alternative arrangements had had to be made for the work to be done abroad, where, as he pointed out, the workers earned 2/- a week less than the Leek dyers and who worked 10-11 hours longer every week. Thomas said that the Churnet Works would definitely have to close for dyeing, and Arthur's chance to be an employer had gone. *"A great loss and no small trouble to my wife and myself."* The trouble-makers were young 20 year olds, insufficiently skilled in any case, and not worthy of an increase in the standard wage. Finally, Thomas accused the trade union secretary, a man called Stubbs, of intimidating those men who still wished to continue working. The meeting broke up with bitterness. Maybe Thomas had tried to invoke some sympathy with the family by his explanation of Arthur's difficulties, but it did not have that effect.

After a couple of weeks, the men came back with a demand for an immediate increase of 1/-, and another 1/- in six months' time. Thomas' reply was an angry refusal. A board of conciliation was set up, but to no effect. It happened that Tom Mann, a nationally famous trade union leader was visiting Leek at this time. He met Thomas, and the two men got on extremely well. Mann apparently received a promise that the wages would be reconsidered if it could be proved that other firms were paying more. The Leek Times had meanwhile been fanning the flames of discontent. It published weekly lists of those who were subscribing to the strike fund, also some vitriolic attacks on blacklegs who went back to work. The paper accused Thomas of intransigence to begin with, and then of changing his arguments. Such heat was engendered by the dispute that it is difficult to assess what the true position was. But it would appear that by Hammersley's own admission, higher wages were indeed being paid to their workers, and Thomas then reneged on his offer. So incensed was Tom Mann at this reversal, that he sent copies of all the correspondence he had had with Thomas to the Leek Times for publication. This naturally gained the Wardles a good deal of unfavourable publicity.

Thomas was always more protective of Arthur than of his other sons, but his handling of the dispute was hardly a good example to the young man of good industrial relations. The Churnet Works did not close despite Thomas' predictions, but still stands today, although no longer in the hands of the Wardle family.

Meanwhile, Elizabeth had been dividing her time between the embroidery school and work for local charities. But in 1891, she uncharacteristically wrote a book. Practical as ever, her one and only literary venture was a cookery book. In 1877, Elizabeth had been Honorary Secretary to the Leek School of Cookery for a couple of years. The experience must have helped her in the compilation of her book. The title was *'366 easy and inexpensive dinners arranged for young house-keepers'*. It was printed both in London and in Leek, dedicated to her daughters, daughters-in-law and grand-daughters, with thanks to her friend and secretary, Miss B.Lowe. In the preface, she said that she married at 22 with no knowledge

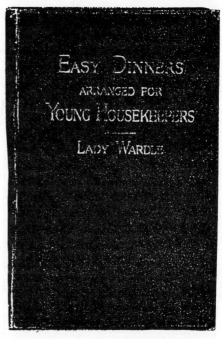

of house-keeping and had inexperienced servants. *"I was weighed down with a burden which I carried with me for at least a year - mystified with cookery books containing recipes requiring ingredients I found a difficulty in procuring, and French dishes not at all suited to a middle-class household."* In order to help a new generation of young housewives, she compiled suggested menus for each day of the year, using the new edition of Mrs Beaton's 'Everyday Cookbook', except where she gave recipes and tips of her own. *"I have provided general homely fare, day by day. The house-keeper should make her own lists for salads and fancy sweets. Before going to market, she should look forward to the proposed dinners for the next seven days and note in a pocket-book the food required...remembering that if there is to be pickled beef it should be ordered three weeks in advance, and saddle of mutton a fortnight in advance. All mutton ought to be QUITE a week old before cooking except in Summer. These dinners are more suitable for the Northern and Midland counties than for the Southern, as in the South the fish are different and the seasons are earlier. "* Vegetables were suggested, but the house-keeper must study the market and buy what is in season. Every seventh midday meal was marked S for Sunday; evening meals were also given except on Sundays. The servants were to have the same food unless otherwise stated.

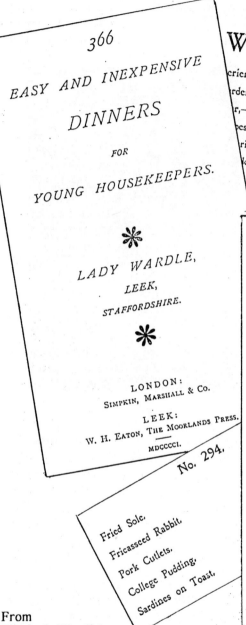

366

EASY AND INEXPENSIVE

DINNERS

FOR

YOUNG HOUSEKEEPERS.

✳

LADY WARDLE,

LEEK,

STAFFORDSHIRE.

✳

LONDON:
SIMPKIN, MARSHALL & Co.

LEEK:
W. H. EATON, THE MOORLANDS PRESS.

MDCCCCI.

No. 294.

Fried Sole.
Fricasseed Rabbit.
Pork Cutlets.
College Pudding.
Sardines on Toast.

From
Elizabeth Wardle's
Cookery Book

PREFACE.

—

WHEN at the age of 22, I married without any knowledge of housekeeping, and having inex- erienced servants, I was weighed down with a rden which I carried with me for at least a r,—mystified with Cookery Books containing es requiring ingredients I found a difficulty in ring, and French dishes not at all suited to dle-class household. In remembrance of that have prepared this little book for the help g wives and housekeepers with limited in-

JANUARY.

—

No. 1.

1 lb. steak of Cod with Oyster Sauce (five or six oysters are enough).

Middle of Neck of Mutton, boiled, with Caper Sauce, Carrots and Turnips.

Mince Pies.

Welsh Rabbit.

No. 2.

Scotch Broth.

Turkey Legs grilled (supposing there will be the remains of a Turkey at Christmas time).

Marmalade Pudding.

Kitchen: 1 lb. Steak stewed, with vegetables.

N.B.—The Broth should be made from the liquor in which the Mutton was stewed, saving some of the boiled carrots and turnips to put into it.

Some of Elizabeth's economical tips were how to make stock, instructions for various puddings, what the butcher can be asked to bone and prepare, and how to warm up cold meat so that it tastes freshly cooked. She included tinned soup and tinned fruit on her menus, while *foie gras*, oysters and lobster feature quite frequently. There is a copy of this book in the Nicholson Institute, but unfortunately no record of how much it was used by the daughters and daughters-in-law. The experience of helping to run the Leek school of cookery nearly twenty years previously must have helped Elizabeth in its compilation.

This was an active time for Thomas in the Field Club, and in his geological pursuits. First of all, he was elected in both 1890 and 1891 to the Council of the Palaentographical Society, to which he had belonged even when he lived at Leekbrook. (Nearly thirty years previously, there had been great excitement over the discovery of some supposed mammoth bones near Waterhouses, and Thomas had been one of the party that set out from Leek to investigate the find. It may well have been the interest and excitement of this expedition that prompted him to join the Society.) The appointment to the Council involved attending three meetings a year to consider the contents and the publishing of the Society's Annual Volume. It was an indication of the regard in which he was held by the palaeontological world despite his amateur status. Proud though he was of the honour, he only attended one Council meeting the first year and none the following one, so it was not surprising that his name was not put forward for re-election in 1892.

He was more active on behalf of the Geologists' Association. When their Summer expedition came to Staffordshire in 1890, Thomas was one of those who planned the route and guided the party, also offering hospitality to one or two of the members, He escorted them to see the Yoredale rocks of Butterton Moor - *"theoretically the best road-making rocks"*, as he described them.

Greatly to his delight, he was elected President of the Field Club in both 1891 and 1892. Having already held the office 20 years earlier, it was an unusual honour to be re-elected twice more. Busy as he was with other matters, he attended all the evening meetings and most of the expeditions during his Presidential years. It was more of a commitment this time - from a membership of 297 when he was first in office in 1872, there were now nearly 400 members, more evening meetings and six or seven 'sections', specialist sub-committees with their own activities. He had been the leader of the geology section ever since it started, also of the microscopy one, though the latter could not have been too demanding since there was only one other member beside himself. He had given no fewer than twelve papers on geology over the years, the highlight being when he discovered the presence of microscopic quartz crystals in limestone, up to 6% of its weight. He had tirelessly produced exhibits for the evening meetings: silk producing lepidoptera; silk and embroideries; Indian craft work and, of course, his fossils. In January 1892 he put on the biggest display of all for the members, producing the whole of the collection of objets d'art that he had brought back from India. The exhibit were arranged with much taste, according to the local paper, in four of the rooms at the Nicholson Institute, ranging from an Indian Prince's tinselled notepaper through fabrics, metal work and stuffed animals to Afghan coats.

For the first of his two Presidential Addresses he chose to speak on the entymology of silk. Although the members had heard him speak about silk on previous occasions – notably, at the time of the Manchester Golden Jubilee Exhibition when he organised a day's outing for them to visit it – this was a particularly good lecture containing a lot of information new to his audience. He described some of the more exotic silk-producing lepidoptera, from a tiny half-inch long caterpillar to the larvae of the tussur moths, two of which he had taken from a terminalia tree in a missionary's garden in the jungle of Bengal, five inches long and three quarters of an inch thick. Some of the African moths first weave a bag and then cluster inside it, each spinning its own cocoon. There were solitary moths and colonising ones, spiders and so-called military worms that walk in single file, one behind the other, (Thomas had found a line of these one day doing a slow march along the hot-water pipes in his greenhouse).

He traced the history of silk from Aristotle and Caesar to the present day, and had borrowed brocades, brocatelles and damasks from Messrs Warner and Sons from Spitalfields and from George Bermingham of Leek, to illustrate the beauty and high quality of modern English silk. He was particularly proud to add to the display a collection of tussur silk tram dyed to the exact colours of fourteen different precious stones by Gilbert.

Naturally, he took the opportunity to try to gain recruits for the Ladies' section of the Silk Association. Paying tribute to the very active support given by the Duchess of Teck, he recalled how she had announced on her daughter's engagement that all the silks for the wedding should be of British manufacture. *"The looms of Spitalfields were merry with the sound of shuttles,"* until the tragic death of the young Prince. He showed a pattern of the silk brocade with silver May blossoms that had been woven by Warner's of Spitalfields for the wedding dress. (When the Princess later married the Duke of York, a similar resurgence of the home industry took place.) This speech with the accompanying display and slides was received extremely well by the club members.

The following year however, when Thomas gave his second presidential address, he chose a much less popular subject: 'Bacteriology'. In it he used much of the material researched for his book on 'Sewage Disposal' which he was in process of writing at the time. As a silk dyer and as a keen fisherman, he had always been interested in the purity of river water (indeed, twenty years earlier he had taken thirty members the Field Club to the Staffordshire Potteries Waterworks and lectured to them in the rain about the pure water supply from the Yoredale series of rocks). The researches into silkworm diseases which he had undertaken in India were the result of his knowledge of bacteriology, so he was no stranger to the subject.

He became increasingly interested in the problem of water pollution. Ever growing urban populations, together with ever increasing industrial waste, had created a serious national situation. Even when it was recognised that bacteria from raw or imperfectly treated sewage caused disease, most local authorities were ill equipped with the money or with the scientific knowledge to deal with the problem effectively. Florence Nightingale is quoted as having said: *"What is the use of praying that London will be free of cholera when every common sewer empties into the Thames?"* When the Thames conservators did publish a standard for the purification of sewage, an expert commented: *"...I wish it to be distinctly understood that in my opinion, effluent of such a standard can only be safely admissable into the Thames on condition that the water is not afterwards used for domestic purposes."* That expert was one of the River Pollution Commissioners who had brought out a report in 1868, setting standards for sewage purification. Their proposed standards were never mandatory, and were only adopted in a few areas for a short time, and then abandoned by the Government as being impractical.

The conditions of London were reflected throughout the country. Every town had to tackle the sewage problem; Leek accordingly had a sanitary committee of the Town Improvement Commissioners, also a sewage enquiry sub-committee. Thomas served on both these bodies, an obvious choice since he was a professional chemist, already skilled in the use of a microscope and well versed in the findings of Pasteur on bacteriology. Having agreed that the present system of waste disposal was inadequate and likely to endanger public health, it was difficult to choose an alternative. There were various irrigation methods in use, also both chemical and electrical precipitation schemes. Indeed, between 1865 and 1875, no fewer than 400 patents were taken out for chemical treatment alone! Thomas commented: *"Throughout the country generally, we find opinions on the treatment and disposal of sewage of a most varied and conflicting character. I do not regard this as a bad sign. I think it shows that everyone is seeking a remedy for an unhealthy state of things and we shall have to come to a common agreement on it..."*

To help the Leek Commissioners to find the best solution for their local situation, Thomas proposed writing to a number of other towns to ask how they were dealing with the problem. He drafted a list of forty questions, which was duly dispatched by the Town Clerk to each of the chosen towns. Fifty five answers were received, which certainly provided sufficient data for a comparative study. The questions included one asking about the percentage of 'privies' as compared to water closets. The answers were very disparate: Leek Rural District apparently had no water closets at all, and yet nearby Buxton was almost entirely provided with them. Some authorities still allowed raw sewage to be put on the land as a fertiliser, although it had been accepted for some years by experts that animals grazing on land thus treated could pass on diseases to the human consumer. Some of the sewage from

Longton was piped onto the Duke of Sutherland's land at Trentham, to fertilise his farms. After this broad irrigation, the effluent outfall into the Trent rendered the river water "decidedly unsanitary", as Thomas put it. (The Duke was paid £750 a year by the Longton Corporation for thus disposing of their sewage for them.)

The next stage was for the committee to visit nearby sewerage works. They went to Fenton, Hanley, Longton and Newcastle, and then decided they had seen enough to be able to choose a system suitable for Leek. But by now, Thomas was full of crusading enthusiasm. Having started merely by trying to compose statistics of methods, costings and efficiency so that the Leek Commissioners could make an informed choice, he found himself so interested in the subject that he continued his investigations on his own. He examined the systems used by at least twelve other towns, also the cities of Birmingham and Manchester. Everywhere he took samples of effluent and made copious notes, and fitted up a special laboratory for his research. He had an assistant, Joseph Lunt, B.Sc., who helped hlm with his analyses and experiments. Thomas' keenness took him to a well-known analytical chemist in London, Hugo Wollheim of Leadenhall Street, where he spent hours having the 'amines' process of sewage treatment demonstrated to him. He went to the Electrical Purification Association in Westminster as well, to see electrolysis being used for precipitation.

So occupied was he with his investigations that be once forgot a gallon stone jar of sewage that had been three months awaiting analysis. In his words: *"It exploded violently with a loud report. The laboratory was immediately filled with a most intolerable stench. The adjoining offices had to be evacuated, all the windows opened, and it was some time before the stench was got rid of..."* As he concluded, if bacterial growth could cause putrefactive gases of such force in only one gallon of sewage, the enormous multiplication of disease-carrying organisms in the imperfectly treated system for a whole town could hardly be imagined. (The staff who had to clear up the mess in his laboratory probably thought it was an unnecessarily practical way to prove his point.)

Thomas became so interested in all the facts he had discovered that he decided to invent his own method for sewage treatment, the Wardle system of ozonine-ferricum. This was a chemical precipitation process, for which a patent was taken out and for which a company was formed to work it – the Standard Sewage and Water Purification Company, with offices in Victoria Street, Manchester and with Thomas as its chairman. When the local Leek paper reported that a tadpole bad been discovered in the Leek tap water, Thomas redoubled his efforts and his book was published in June 1893. By that time, his method was being used at the Salford Corporation sewage works where 100,000 gallons were treated every day, and also at Nuneaton, where the whole of the waste matter was processed by the Wardle method.

But between the writing of his book and its publication, something went wrong. At the beginning, a notice in red is inserted which reads: *"Since this book was printed, I have found it necessary to withdraw my Patented Precipitancy Process and my connection from the Standard Sewage Company mentioned on p.160. Consequently it will be necessary that any communications or consultations which any of my readers may require of me should be made to me direct, addressed Thos. Wardle, Leek."* And on p.160, there was another red notice to the same effect. Whatever the cause for this, it must have been a considerable disappointment to Thomas, and a great annoyance after working on the project for upwards of three years. There was no further mention of his involvement in the subject.

The book was extremely technical, full of statistics, chemical formulae and illustrations of bacterial microscopic slides. But even to a reader unversed in such matters, many points of interest were to be found. First, it was dedicated *"with sincere esteem to my old friend and schoolfellow, Charles Lowe, Esq., F.C.S."* Ever since their days at Birch Grove School in Macclesfield, the two men had kept up their friendship. Their children had spent holidays together, and the families visited regularly. Charles Lowe had made a career as a research chemist, and although not so well known as Thomas had become, he was an extremely successful and wealthy business man. It must have seemed an appropriate choice to dedicate the book to an old friend, and, moreover, to one who would understand it.

It is also of interest that Thomas was already interested in the problems of waste disposal when he visited India. He could not resist a description of what he had seen out there: *"The sewage and garbage disposal arrangements of Calcutta which I carefully examined on the spot, are simply horrible. They consist solely in running them into a huge canal, where numbers of animals of various kinds lie decomposing...the garbage train is so laden with putrefactive matter that it is one of the most wonderful of sights to see the cloud of vultures and other huge scavenger birds which gather and soon cover the wagons.....the air is simply charged with putrefactive germs and odours. It was several days before I recovered from my visit to this place."*

In 1894, shortly after the publication of Thomas' book, many dead grayling and trout were reported in the Churnet river due to sewage pollution, and at Stone, dead fish were seen for days after a discharge from a 'manufactuary' upstream. While the sanitary committee tried to decide the best way to deal with the problem, the North Staffordshire Field Club made its contribution by setting up a system of reporting on the condition of watercourses and the fish in them. Both Thomas and his son Fred helped with these reports. The new Club President remarked on the gravity and urgency of the situation in his address: *"Our President of last year, Mr Wardle, is to be congratulated on his noble endeavours in this field. The County Council and the sanitary authorities are now alive to the danger and it is to be hoped that streams will soon be purer once again, with fish available for food and for sport."*

Congratulations for a different reason were soon to be offered once again to Thomas by his successor. The Field Club at the 1896 Annual Meeting bestowed on him its highest honour; the Garner Medal. This was awarded from time to time, in memory of a past President, to a member for outstanding original work. In Thomas' case it was given for his contributions on the Entymology of Silk and on the Geology of North Staffordshire. This was a rare distinction from a club holding the highest reputation for research and original thought in the Midlands, and Thomas was sincerely gratified.

The Autumn outing for the club was arranged by Thomas, when nearly fifty members went on an excursion to Eccleshall. They were met by carriages at Norton Bridge station and taken to see the remains of the castle at Eccleshall, then conducted round the church where G.E.Street had been the architect for the restoration. The next item on the programme was for them to travel the 2½ miles to Sugnall Hall, which had recently been bought by Thomas' friend, Charles Lowe. His main family home was in Knutsford and he owned a house in Wales at Barmouth, where the Wardle boys had spent many happy holidays, but Sugnall was his latest acquisition. After they had enjoyed some refreshment, the party visited two sites of interest on the Sugnall estate on their return journey to Eccleshall; a sandstone quarry, and the lake, Copmere. Copmere was covered with a mantle of bright green algae that afternoon, a phenomenon not unusual on meres, but something the members had not seen before. Thomas had visited the lake several times previously when it was perfectly clear, but he had heard about the algae which covered the surface sometimes in late Summer or early Autumn and he was as intrigued as everyone else to see it for himself. He took samples of the water and analysed them when he got home. Fascinated by the two different types of plant material he discovered, he prepared a paper illustrated with slides for the Microscopy Section of the Club. The 'breaking' of the mere (a local name for the turbidity) had two undesirable effects; the fish suffered, and when the vegetable matter was decaying there was a most unpleasant smell. Charles Lowe had been hopeful that his friend, with all his bacteriological experience, would be able to advise on some method of curing it. But although Thomas studied the water, the chlorophyll and the plant material, he could not explain why it happened some years and not others, and in some pools and not others even when they shared the same water source. However, when his paper was presented at Trentham it aroused much interest and was a reminder of a particularly enjoyable excursion.

Despite his three years concentrating on sewage disposal, the affairs of the Silk Association necessarily still took much of Thomas' time. The Indian Government did not forget its undertaking to supply the Association with information that might be useful to the members. For instance, a paper arrived on what the Madras Government was doing to develop Tussur production, also a monograph on silk in the Punjab, both of which were duly circulated to the members. Thomas reciprocated by sending the latest circulars and instruction books on Italian silk rearing: *"I thought I had better send you one of each as they may be useful to India."* Since they were in

Italian, there is no means of knowing how useful they were, but for his Silk Association members Thomas translated them and had them published in the Leek Times.

Various sub-committees of the Association had been appointed to study and report on matters of concern for the silk industry, including one to examine the development of power looms. Thomas was very active in the research and wrote a booklet on the subject in 1893, dedicated to the Duchess of Teck. The object of the report was to impress on English manufacturers what rapid developments had taken place in power loom weaving on the Continent and the urgent need to modernise their methods. The information had mainly been gathered by Thomas after visiting his old manufacturing friends in Lyons. He quoted figures for the price of looms, the daily output, the speed of shuttles per minute and the wages paid to the machine operators. Mechanisation had brought silk weaving into a factory situation, very different from the early days of handweaving when it was a cottage industry with the weavers having their own looms and working from their own homes. Always interested in new technology, Thomas was plainly impatient at the failure of the British industrialists to keep up with the times and to invest in powered machinery.

The need to keep English silk in the eye of the public was still a priority for the Association. Accordingly, Thomas felt that after the second exhibition in London, it was time to try one in the provinces. One year after Stafford House, in 1895 a show took place in Stafford itself, at the Borough Hall. It was opened by H.R.H. the Duchess of Teck in the presence of Sir Oswald Moseley, then High Sheriff of Staffordshire, and the Duchess of Sutherland. This time, Thomas varied the exhibits between silks, ancient and modern embroideries and a display of drawings from the collection of William Brough. There was also promotional literature for the Ladies' Silk Association, urging those "interested in the prosperity of this National Industry" to enrol. There were 62 stands, including exhibits from Debenham and Freebody, Courtaulds, Brookfields of Stafford, Joshua Wardle and Sons and the Leek Embroidery Society. The most outstanding item on the last mentioned display was an embroidered dossal designed by Gerald Horsley; three angels with 'Alleluia' embedded in foliage and flowers. Some of the antique embroideries were provided by Thomas himself, such as a reliquary cover of Persian weaving. An item which greatly interested the public was a tablecloth worked by Queen Adelaide, the property of Mrs Salt of Standon Rectory. It was a five day exhibition – a successful one, though evidently not without its problems: *"Several of the exhibits have arrived too late to be catalogued"*; (a copy of the catalogue is in the Salt Library in Stafford).

Shortly after the Stafford Exhibition, Thomas was asked to make an advisory report on the silk industry of Cyprus by Joseph Chamberlain, then Secretary of State for the Colonies. Ten years previously, he had examined cocoons and raw silk from Cyprus at the Colonial and Indian Exhibition in London, and had given them high praise. No notice had been taken at the time of his recommendation that steps should be taken to revive the silk production of the island. Subsequent further decline had led the High Commissioner, Sir Hugh Sendall, to ask the British Government that a new appraisal be made of the ancient silk industry.

To make his report, Thomas had his previous notes and some silk products sent by the High Commissioner for his examination. He tested seven different types of cocoons, and still held to the opinion that the fibres were the strongest he had ever seen, with the greatest average diameter of any. They would be eminently suitable for the manufacture of sewing silks. His conclusion was that Cyprus could be just as important as Italy in high grade Bombyx Mori production, and that the moribund industry was well worth saving. He recommended that a government sericulturalist should be appointed *"to teach the natives how properly to cultivate the mulberry, how to breed silkworms free from disease, and better reeling."* To preserve the indigenous race of worms, he suggested that the entire output of cocoons be kept for breeding until stocks were up to strength, rather than importing foreign eggs to increase supplies. Finally, he suggested that in the more mountainous parts of the island where oak trees abounded, there should be an experimental area for introducing Chinese oak-leaf eating tussur worms.

Much to his annoyance, his report was sent for comment to the Director of Kew Gardens, Thistleton-Dyer. Thomas had previously corresponded quite frequently with this gentleman on friendly terms, but was highly indignant when he learned that Thistleton-Dyer had criticised his suggestions. He wrote several months later to the Secretary of State: *"...my proposals have been quite misunderstood in several respects. For instance, Mr. Dyer says we had better cultivate Chinese silkworms in Cyprus. I excuse him for this view because he is not a silk expert..."* Only an experimental tussur area had been suggested, but Dyer's comments had prevented the purchase of eggs for the purpose for the current year, and delayed a start on the breeding of the indigeneous species.

There had been a proposal to send Thomas out to Cyprus to see the situation at first hand, but he wrote: *"If there is to be no continuity or permanent outcome of my visit to Cyprus beyond a few years' trials, I should prefer not to go. It is a useless expenditure sending me out if the trials are to be upset by the next change of government or the varying views of different Governors."* It was rare for Thomas to decline an opportunity to travel, but he had been annoyed at a second opinion being sought, and his experience in India was still rankling. Having given his professional opinion and demolished Mr Dyer's criticisms, he left the matter for the politicians to decide.

From Kashmir, however, there was news of progress. Colonel Nisbet had been replaced as Resident by Sir Adelbert Talbot, who was equally keen to encourage a revival of the silk indutry. Having read the Wardle correspondence and reports, Sir Adelbert strongly advised the Maharajah that more positive steps were needed. For one thing, although Mukerjee was doing his best, a practical expert with knowledge of modern methods was required to organise the whole operation, together with up–to–date machinery and new silk seed from abroad that was free of all disease.

A request from Kashmir was duly received in London for help in these matters and Thomas was asked to advise. Needless to say, Thomas was delighted to be consulted. Regarding the appointment of a sericulturalist, the Kashmir Government first asked him to recommend a Frenchman or an Italian, knowing that both countries had experts at their respective Silk Institutes. Thomas, however, was not happy to recommend either nationality – partly because he did not know anyone suitably experienced to fill the post, and partly because he felt it would be a mistake to appoint someone who could speak neither English nor any Indian dialect. He did know of a Mr.Walton, whom he had met when he was in India. This man had wide experience in the filatures in Bengal, spoke the native language, and Thomas happened to know that he was unemployed at that time. After many official telegrams, Mr.Walton went to Kashmir for an interview and was straightaway given the job. It proved to be an excellent appointment. Walton was a good organiser, knowledgeable about modern methods and he responded with enthusiasm to the challenge of reviving the Kashmiri silk industry.

Sir George Birdwood had not been entirely happy about Thomas' suggestion of Mr.Walton. He wrote: *"I do not like giving up the proposal to employ an Italian, nor do I like employing a middle-aged Englishman who is hampered with a family on so important an undertaking as the revival from the ground of the Kashmir silk industry. Mr Walton is 45 and has a wife and three children. But he is a gentleman with good Indian connections and of course this is a great point when engaging a European who has to work with other English gentlemen for employment in a native state. If he is not in a position to eat salt with the sahibs, he will lose influence and inevitably gravitate into a position of antagonism towards the English officers of state and become involved in the puerile intrigues which are the curse of most native courts. If we do have to fall back on an Italian, I have made it clear that he is to be a thorough gentleman,"* (an interesting comment on the days of the British Raj). Although he had initial misgivings about Mr Walton, Sir George came to appreciate the excellent job he did in Kashmir.

Before the next step was taken in response to the request from Kashmir – that was, the purchase of new machinery and seed – Thomas had decided to take a big step in his private life. He had long dreamed of having a small house as a country retreat, and by 1896 he felt his financial position to be sufficiently secure for this to be possible. After a gruelling business schedule during the week, he wanted somewhere peaceful for weekends, in the North Staffordshire Moorlands which he loved. Moreover, to have a shooting or fishing lodge was very fashionable, a sign of having 'arrived' socially. The house he decided to buy was Swainsley Hall, overlooking the Manifold valley, nine miles from Leek. It had been built in 1867 by a solicitor from London called Roscoe. For Thomas' large family, it needed some alterations and he extended it on the west side before starting to spend weekends there during the Summer of 1896.

Thomas and Elizabeth were delighted with their new 'country cottage' and furnished it with many of the acquisitions from India. He had a considerable art collection by now, so he took all his drawings and prints by Rossetti to Swainsley, where one room was called the Rossetti room and was reputed to house 50 examples of the artist's work When an old house in Leek that had belonged to the Joliffe family was pulled down, Thomas bought the panelling and installed it at Swainsley. To complete the ideal 'retreat', there had to be an organ, for music had always been one of the family's favourite forms of recreation. One of the downstairs rooms became the organ room, with a wooden loft above. Typically of Thomas the instrument was driven by the power of the river, harnessed by him. Outside, in true Victorian fashion, Thomas cultivated a fernery in the garden and bred ornamental pheasants.

Always hospitable, Thomas took a delight in entertaining his friends at Swainsley. One of the first to be invited to visit it was William Morris, but – as has been mentioned in a previous chapter – Morris was already too ill to travel and died very soon after receiving Thomas' letter of invitation. Among the steady stream of guests was Samuel Langhorne Clemens, better known as the writer Mark Twain, whose visit was featured in the Leek Post. Another distinguished visitor was General Sir Robert Baden-Powell, who insisted on arrival that he did not need a bedroom as he always slept out of doors. He accordingly pitched the tent he had brought with him in a nearby field and slept there on a camp bed during his stay.

Many friends remembered their visits to Swainsley with much pleasure; shooting and fishing friends, silk associates and geological colleagues. One of the latter was Edward Hull, who wrote about the Wardle hospitality in his autobiography *'Reminiscences of a Strenuous Life'*. He had met Thomas when he was doing the geological survey of Lancashire and they had remained friends ever since.

Now that he spent much time near the River Manifold, Thomas gave it some special attention. The peculiarity of the river is that it disappears when the weather is dry through fissures in its bed, called the swallowholes, and runs underground beneath its own course for several miles from Wetton to Ilam, where it emerges into the open again. Various people, including the historian Dr Plot, and Dr Johnson, had speculated in the past as to whether the water that appeared out of the Boil Holes at Ilam was indeed the same river that disappeared at Wetton Mill. This Thomas proved to be so, by using a harmless dye. Geologically, of course, this pervious character of the river was fascinating to him. But the dry pebbles of the surface bed was unattractive to look at, and a hardship to the farmers who depended on the Manifold to water their cattle. So Thomas decided to make an experiment; he plugged the Swallowholes with concrete so that the river would stay above ground all Summer. The Field Club was told of his scheme, and wished him well at one of the meetings. But the River Manifold was not going to allow its nature to be changed by Thomas. It was said that the noise of the plug being blown out was like a clap of thunder, and the neighbourhood talked about the explosion for years. The river resumed its pervious way, but Thomas did not attempt to alter it again.

When the family spent weekends at Swainsley, they worshipped at Warslow church, where Thomas played the organ and trained the choir when he had time. But when the construction of the Manifold and District Light Railway was under way, large quantities of stone were excavated from Ecton quarry for railroad use and Thomas had a little mission chapel built at Ecton with some of the stone left over. Ecton was much nearer to Swainsley than Warslow, and therefore more convenient for the Wardles. The chapel was extremely small and so was the congregation, but Thomas bought a harmonium for it and Elizabeth saw that it had Leek embroidery furnishings.

Thomas relaxed at Swainsley and became more genial than he had been for a long time. The journey from Leek was by horse drawn transport, usually in a trap with a chestnut pony called Charlie. There was a family story that all Thomas needed to do when leaving 54 St Edward Street in Leek was to say *"Swainsley, Charlie"*, tie the reins to the trap and Charlie would take over for the nine mile journey.

Reminiscences by a fishing friend of Thomas give a good picture of life at Swainsley about this time: *"It was at his country house.....that my friend was seen at his best and happiest. Here was a hall crammed full of trophies brought back from India, including a huge Bengal tiger. Here were reminders of Scottish salmon fishing expeditions, a rack of many fly rods, drawers full of flies, a room devoted to chemical and microscopic work, a fine organ, the bellows of which – and this was characteristic of the man – were blown by water power elevated from the Manifold by means of a hydraulic ram. On the walls hung drawings and other relics of Morris and Rossetti."* Days at Swainsley, he went on, are joyful memories. The soft music of the distant organ played by his host who was as a rule a most early riser, would rouse the fly-fishing guest and send him springing out of bed to look down the valley and glance skywards to gauge the weather prospects for the day. At the cheery breakfast, in a room surrounded with Indian curiosities and works of art, the plan of campaign against the trout and grayling would be discussed. During the hours of morning, which often had to be devoted to an enormous correspondence, the thoughtful host would send his guest up the Manifold, a bewitching little stream of many bends (hence its name), from which it was no difficult matter to secure from six to a dozen brace of trout. Or there might be a visit to the aviary where pheasants of many kinds were kept, and where at one time there was an extremely hungry trained cormorant, which one June morning *"attacked my foot and endeavoured to swallow it."*

There is a relic of those happy times the other side of the Manifold River from Swainsley, on Ecton Hill. This was the highest point that Thomas could see from his study, and he built an 8-10 foot tower there which he jokingly called 'Wardlestein'. Only about 3 feet of the tower now remains and it can barely be seen, but it had been the family 'folly'.

Another family joke still remembered was that when a dish of trout was on the menu, Thomas would phrase the Grace; *"For all His MANIFOLD blessings may the Lord's name be praised",* said with a twinkle in his eye.

The Warslow Window

A selection of alms bags from Warslow Church

The little chapel at Ecton (on the right), where Thomas played the organ.

The Cottage Hospital, Leek.
Thomas Wardle was Chairman of the of the Cottage Hospital Supporters in the 1890's/

One of Captain Byrom's Shooting Parties at Abbey Farm, Abbey Green, Leek, c1895.
(William Richard Colin Jones Byrom, b.1864)
The gentlemen seated with guns, L to R:
Gilbert Wardle, Edward Challinor, Marcus Prince, Capt Byrom, Sir Thomas Wardle, Dr Hammersley, Victor & Sam Prince

An early view of Swainsley Hall

Swainsley Hall 1950's

Entrance Hall and staircase, Swainsley Hall c 1950

The panelled library, Swainsley Hall c 1950

Gilbert Charles Wardle

Right: Mr & Mrs Gilbert Wardle attending a
wedding at Cheddleton Church

The Churnet Works today.

Lady Wardle presented at court at the investiture of her husband. An evening top made of the fabric of this gold brocade dress still remains in the family.

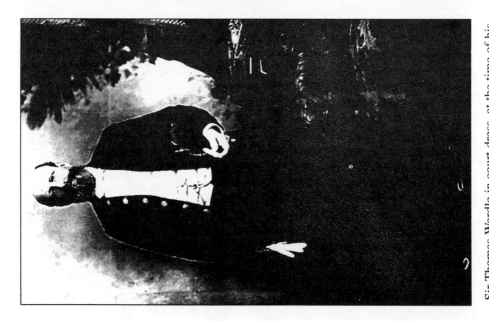

Sir Thomas Wardle in court dress, at the time of his presentation. S G Worthington now holds this outfit in a tin trunk at Blore. Sword, shoes etc remain intact.

Chapter Eight

THE KNIGHT AND WIDOWER

January lst, 1897, was one of the high spots in the story of the Wardles. In the Queen's New Year's Honours List, it was announced that Thomas had been given a knighthood for his services to the silk industry. The honour was awarded 'at the instance of Lord Salisbury', who had started Thomas on the way to the top many years previously by asking him to write his report on the 'Dyes and Tans of India'. The pride and pleasure of the family can be imagined. In the William Salt Library, Stafford, there is a printed card dated Leek, January 7th, which reads: "Mr and Mrs Wardle desire to return thanks to all friends who have so kindly sent congratulations and good wishes on the occasion of Mr Wardle's name being included in the list of Her Majesty's New Year's Honours." Typical of the messages received was that from the Field Club: "...seldom has honour been better deserved or more worthily given."

There is a picture in the Leek Annual for 1898 of Thomas in his court dress for the investiture: black silk suit with knee breeches, hat under his arm, black silk stockings and silver buckles on his shoes. He looked extremely distinguished, and that year his name headed the Directory, together with that of the Duchess of Sutherland. The court dress is still in excellent condition in the possession of one of his great-grandsons.

Amid the family's rejoicing, there was still work to be done. Before January was over, Thomas was called upon by the Silk Association to lead a delegation to the Prince of Wales, asking H.R.H. to help British industry by supporting a revival of the fashion of silk waistcoats for gentlemen's evening wear. The Prince, as was reported in the press, 'readily accorded his support', much to the pleasure of the Association.

A more serious but less successful campaign, spearheaded by Thomas, requested the Manchester Municipal School of Technology to provide courses on silk dyeing and weaving. These efforts were mainly on behalf of the silk manufacturers of Macclesfield, but as they were not prepared to pay towards the cost of running such courses, the requests came to nothing. Over the years, Thomas had become well-known in Manchester, and not only for his Chairmanship of the Silk Association. Since 1895, he had been a governor of the Whitworth Art Gallery, and later on he became a Council member as well. He was on the building committee, responsible for planning the new galleries which were opened in 1908, and also on the Art Committee. He was a regular attender at the meetings until the last two years of his life, often recorded as requesting the loan of something for an exhibition in which he had an interest; Kincobs (Indian brocades) and silks for the Indian Jubilee Exhibition at the Crystal Palace in 1897, paintings for a display in Macclesfield, and a large Indian screen together with some etchings for the Nicholson Institute in Leek.

In March 1897, Thomas was in both Manchester and Macclesfield, lecturing on the chemical weighting of silk, a practice of which he had always been critical. He was joined in these lectures by Mr Carter-Bell, Honorary Chemist to the Silk Association, and the text was published the following year as a guide to manufacturers.

When raw silk had been 'boiled off' to remove the seracin (or natural gum), its weight was reduced by as much as 25%. Although the process was necessary if the silk was to be bright and lustrous, the manufacturers were loathe to loose a quarter of the bulk of their valuable product by this means. In the eighteenth century sugar had been used to adulterate the silk, thereby increasing its weight. Later, the old sugar treatment had been superceded by chemical methods. The silk, both 'boiled off' and 'in the gum', was immersed in vegetable extracts containing tannic acid. This caused the fibres to expand and thicken, thereby greatly increasing the bulk of the silk. More recently, experiments were made with various metallic salts, such as tin and lead. Indeed, as Thomas told his audiences, *"no dye house is now complete without its laboratory. The dyer needs both organic and inorganic chemistry, not so much for tinctorial purposes as for swelling the fibre by chemicals. There can be up to 400% adulteration by these means."*

English dyers did not weight their silk to the same extent as their Continental counterparts, which had partly been responsible for our silks being more expensive. Some English houses did sell only pure silk, while others weighted to a moderate degree so that they could compete with foreign prices. But the European dyers were adulterating the silk to such an extent that, according to Thomas, *"the very nature of silk was threatened and the market endangered"*. The effects of over-weighting caused silk to crack or tear after very little use, also to make the dye come out, as in the case of the sailors' neckerchiefs. The adulteration had reached such a state in Zurich that silk merchants had to advertise that they would replace any silk taffeta that had gone into holes. Bridal dresses, said Thomas, had been known to fall to pieces like tinder; customers had been asked to report dresses that tore at the folds after only a few wearings. There was only one consolation to the customer, in the fact that heavily weighted silk is incombustible, inclined to smoulder rather than to flare up.

Finally, the dyers of Crefeld in Germany decided that the extreme overweighting must be stopped in the interests of the silk trade as a whole. They conferred with dyers from Zurich and elsewhere, and agreed on a code of practice enforcable by very severe penalties on those who ignored it. This new code was to be introduced in late April, which was why Thomas and his colleague had been asked to explain the details to the English silk manufacturers before it came into force.

The excitement of his knighthood, and the urgency of preparing the home industry for the new weighting regulations, had not deflected Thomas from his correspondence with the India Office. Although he had finally given up the idea of an Imperial Silk Research Institute, he still thought he could stimulate silk production by pressure on the India Office. He wrote twice in January and again in March: the price for Bengali silk had more than doubled in the last twelve months since the reeling had been improved, and the demand for it had outstripped the supply – buyers were having to wait for their orders until the November harvest had been reeled. Thomas prefaced his letters by saying he was keeping the India Office up to date with the latest developments with his short progress reports. Although he was thanked politely for them and was assured that they would be passed on to the Government of India, the internal memo read: *"I am anxious that these communications from Mr Wardle should cease. He should be told to address the Government of India direct on the subject."* The India Office was still unwilling to be involved in any commercial development of the silk industry.

Meanwhile from Kashmir, further letters had arrived from Mr Walton, with requests for various purchases for the new silk season. He asked for seed, for machinery, 4–6 reeling machines and 50 tavelettes. Also on the shopping list was a microscope (which Thomas bought at Messrs Beck of Cornhill Street, declaring that the cost of a suitable one would not be more than £10–£12). The Assistant Resident of Kashmir, Captain Chenevix-Trench, was coming home on leave and had been empowered to make the purchases for Kashmir, in consultation with Thomas. After lengthy letters and negotiations, it was agreed that the two men should go together to France and Italy in May, their travelling expenses to be paid by the Government of Kashmir. Arthur Godley wrote to Thomas: *"Both Captain Chenevix-Trench and yourself will be granted 1st class travel expenses and a subsistence allowance at the rate of one guinea a day for the period during which you may be engaged on this deputation, which it is understood will not exceed a fortnight. A joint account of your proceedings, together with the account of expenses incurred, should be furnished to this office at your earliest convenience."*

Thomas replied: *"...I shall start on the journey on Friday or Monday next. I am very closely engaged in my business just now, and I must endeavour to compress my journey within the shortest possible time, but you may rely on my not hurrying it over to the detriment of the duty entrusted to me....I see my subsistence allowance has been fixed at £1 a day, the same as Captain Chenevix-Trench. In doing this, it must have been overlooked that I am not in the pay of the Indian Government, but engaged in an independent business of my own, which I cannot quit without incurring far greater sacrifice than even the most liberal subsistence allowance could possibly repay. Among business people such services as I am now rendering to the India Office would be paid for, beyond out-of-pocket expenses incurred, by an honorarium, but considering the relations on which I have always stood with the India Office, I say nothing of that, and only refer to the matter at all in the frankness engendered by my past friendly relations with the India Office, and the gratifying way in which they have recently been acknowledged. But I cannot accept a subsistence allowance on which I could barely subsist, and, if I am paid at all, must claim 2 guineas a day, or whatever may be the highest sum allowed by the India Office to specialists not in their regular employ."*

Thomas won that round; Arthur Godley replied that 2 guineas would be allowed, and also he would have discretion as to the number of machines purchased as long as the total expenditure did not exceed £200.

In mid-May Thomas duly arrived in Milan and was met by Captain Chenevix-Trench, who had been holidaying on the French Riviera. Since the silk growing season was already well advanced, they decided not to buy any seed for the current year. Instead, they agreed to purchase a selection of cocoons and send them to Kashmir so that Mr Walton could make his own choice when ordering. The two men visited six different silk merchants in Milan and two in France, buying cocoons from each so that a comparative selection could be made. (In compiling the collection, Thomas kept a duplicate set for himself.) At all the companies they visited, they were advised that the order for the new seed needed to be despatched in August for arrival in Kashmir one month later, packed in wooden boxes full of holes and covered in zinc. They were warned that the seed should not be packed in ice nor to exposed to frost, and should be kept in a cool, fresh atmosphere until the following Spring.

Next came the purchase of machinery, which was much more complicated. Before he set out, Thomas had written to the India Office stressing the importance of investing in the latest and very best machinery available. The Chinese and Japanese producers were using new methods and equipment, so it was vital that the infant industry in Kashmir should be provided with equally efficient machinery. A concession was made to the India Office's economical strictures; only a small number of the latest reeling machines and tavelettes would be bought, as they could be reproduced in Kashmir by local craftsmen. In choosing the most suitable equipment, it had to be borne in mind that neither steam power nor electricity were available in Kashmir. The bassines which held the hot water in which the cocoons were softened needed to be heated by a wood fire underneath, and turned by hand.

From Milan they went to Padua to inspect more machinery, and thence to France. Thomas must have spoken both languages fluently, judging by the discussions he reported and the comments he made on the sericultural manuals he brought back with him. It was decided to order two sets of machinery from Italy and one from France, to be sent direct to Mr Walton in Srinagar. All the firms they visited advised them that Kashmir should consider introducing steam power, as it was infinitely better for the reeling process. Wood fire heat was not sufficiently regular, and also created dust which prevented the silk from being truly lustrous. Armed with cocoons, price lists, working drawings, photographs and instruction leaflets, Thomas and Captain Trench returned home. By the beginning of June their report was received by the India Office.

Once again, there was trouble over the reimbursement of expenses, the India Office having decided that there were mistakes in Thomas' accounts. But this time the internal memo read differently to that of ten years previously: *"It is not desirable to dispute the accounts. I still submit that he be paid in full. His services were especially engaged in this matter. Whatever irregularities his bill may present, his actual expenses certainly exceeded them."* Accordingly, Thomas' account for £91.15. 4 was paid only two months later, at the beginning of August.

The payment of the expenses greatly incensed both men. Captain Trench was angry when he discovered that Thomas had received double his own subsistence allowance. He complained bitterly to the India Office, but was told sternly that he was not entitled to any more. And Thomas was upset to discover that neither his report or the sample cocoons had been sent to Mr.Walton because the India Office were still waiting for the bills and dispatch notes for the Italian machinery. He felt it was a most unreasonable delay, bearing in mind the urgency of ordering the seed by the end of August for the coming season. Accordingly, he took matters into his own hands. He immediately sent a copy of his report to Srinagar, together with his own duplicate set of cocoons, and then ordered the new seed himself. Sir George Birdwood was aghast when he learned that Thomas had spent over £600 on silk worm eggs. *"The Government of India would not be likely to foot such a bill..."* Unrepentant, Thomas said he would pay for them himself if necessary. He had taken great care to buy eggs guaranteed free from disease, and was convinced that the time had come to launch out into large scale rearing. He was proved right, as the hatching of the eggs and rearing of the new worms was a great success, and completely healthy. Since his appointment, Mr.Walton had made every preparation necessary in advance. He had instructed the natives on how to build satisfactory rearing huts in their villages, planted new mulberry trees and constructed more filatures (i.e.reeling factory buildings). The first year that Thomas' European seed was used, the production was so good that all the capital outlay was recouped, and he was asked to order £1500 worth of seed for the next year. This was increased to £3040 in 1899 and to £4000 in 1900.

Since pebrine and other silk worm diseases were still endemic in Kashmir, Thomas insisted that they must continue to import fresh European eggs annually, which had been guaranteed free from infection. These were distributed to villagers in the Spring, and by 1901 an estimated 25,000 people were engaged in rearing silk worms in the area. All the reeling was done centrally at Srinagar, using the latest equipment brought back from France and Italy.

In what even Thomas described as a voluminous correspondence with Mr.Walton, he kept in touch with every aspect of the new industry. The silk was Bombyx Mori, the most popular silk of commerce. But Thomas had learned that oak trees abounded in one part of Kashmir. He therefore suggested, as he had done for Cyprus, that Chinese oak-leaf eating tussur worms should be introduced experimentally into that region. He wrote to the India Office about it, but the experiment does not seem to have flourished, if indeed it ever got off the ground. As he admitted, Tussur would never supplant the Bombyx Mori in quality or popularity, but it was strong, pliable and cheaper, and was particularly in demand for embroidery and its spun waste for furniture velvets. (The manufacturers at Lyons were producing new and very attractive brocades using tussur for the weft and cotton for the warp.) Thomas felt that there would be no trouble selling any tussur produced, and it would have exploited the natural supply of oak trees. But Mr.Walton had insufficient trained staff to be able to oversee another project, and the India Office was not interested, so nothing came of the scheme.

Soon after his return from the continent, Thomas had invited the Field Club to Swainsley. So delighted was he with his new country home that he had offered to organise the July expedition in order to show it to his fellow members. A party of 80 met in Leek on the appointed date. First, they were shown a Celtic cross in St.Edward's churchyard, which had been restored by Thomas. William Brough was ill that day, but asked that the members should still see round his garden as planned. Then the party was taken to Swainsley via Morridge and Ecton by seven 'conveyances'. They were met by most of the Wardle family: Thomas and Elizabeth, daughters Lydia, Edith and Lizzie, Bernard and his wife, and Fred. (Arthur and his wife were not present even though they lived nearby at Warslow.) Elizabeth had arranged for a plentiful tea to be laid out for them in two marquees on the lawn, while the Warslow Band provided music. Thomas had plenty for everyone to see; fireflies from the Rhine forests, a live frog-eating snake, three different species of trout swimming in a tank, fossils and a display of Indian craftwork. It must have been a beautiful day as the meeting itself was held on the lawn in front of the house. Thomas read a paper about the Joliffe family of Leek, onetime owners of the house in which Elizabeth's great-grandfather, Ralph Leeke, had lived. The Joliffe family's old town house, dating from 1627, had been pulled down the previous year in the centre of Leek. It had been used as a dress shop and as a saddlery after it ceased to be a private residence and was in a bad state of disrepair by the time it was demolished. But Thomas, ever the conservationist (and ever open to a bargain) had bought the panelling and installed it at Swainsley. He also bought a magnificent plaster ceiling which he presented to the Town Council. Later, the ceiling was put in the new Leek Technical School. The comment in the Field Club journal was: *"..one of the most enjoyable excursions ever organised by the Club"*.

His commitments meant that Thomas needed to make frequent visits to London. For instance, his duties as both an acting and a consultative examiner to the City and Guilds Institute for silk dyeing, throwing and weaving, regularly caused him to spend time in the capital. For some years he had belonged to the Constitutional Club in Northumberland Avenue, where he could stay overnight when necessary. He was also one of the first Fellows of the Imperial Institute when it opened in 1893. The annual subscription was

£2, which entitled members to use the library, billiard room, reading room, refreshment room, etc. and to attend lectures and concerts. There is no record of how much he made use of these facilities, most of which were duplicated at the Constitutional Club. The prestigious standing of the new Institute must have influenced him to wish to join it; also the hope that its journal and its building might have proved useful to the Silk Association. As it happened, no Association article ever appeared in the journal, and the exhibition which Thomas had hoped could be held there had to be cancelled because the building was not completed in time. However in due course, he finally held a special position at the Imperial Institute when he was appointed its Honorary Silk Expert Referee in 1908.

During one of his stays in London, Thomas visited the Foreign Office on behalf of the Silk Associatiion to arrange for a splendid collection of Japanese and Italian silk to be exhibited throughout the country. The Association managed to book the exhibition to be shown in Leek, Macclesfield, Coventry, Bradford, Manchester and Glasgow, where it aroused much interest. After it had toured the country, it was hoped to use it as a nucleus for a textile museum, but this does not seem to have transpired.

Many distinctions came to Thomas after his knighthood. On the academic side, he became a member of the Appointments Board of Cambridge University. In Leek, he was appointed a magistrate. It was quite customary in those days for a Justice to be appointed late in life, when he had attained a position of distinction. According to the records, Thomas was an assiduous attender at court for the first five years, though his attendences became less frequent after that. There were other local responsibilities as well. He was chairman of the Leek Cottage Hospital Supporters, and President of the Literary and Mechanics Instiute. He also contributed £100 towards the new School of Art, Science and Tecnicology, one of the largest contributions received.

Another of Thomas' great interests in Leek was the Spun Silk Company. It had been founded in 1884 by a consortium of Leek silk manufacturers, with Thomas as one of its first directors. Seal cloth had become so popular, the industry recognised that the spinning of silk waste was big business. A Mr.Watson had started a spun silk business in 1880, and it was his factory which was taken over by the consortium. To Thomas, it must have seemed like retributive justice, for Mr.Watson had been in legal dispute with the Wardle works over the weight reduction of his raw silk after being dyed. He had lost the case, and then gone to court again to appeal against the costs awarded against him. He lost that case too, describing Thomas in court as 'a man I have not spoken to for years'. For a considerable time the dispute had been an aggravation to the Wardle brothers, so it must have seemed ironic that it was the Watson works that the new spun silk enterprise took over. The company did well. By 1899, it was paying a dividend of 7½%. That year Thomas was asked to go to Switzerland to represent the directors of the Leek company on a tour of the Swiss spun silk centres. No doubt his proficiency in languages was one of the reasons he was chosen to go. He might also have combined it with his annual visit to Crefeld in Germany, where he inspected the work of the dyeing and design students.

Many accolades continued to come Thomas's way following his knighthood. One that gave him pleasure was an article in 'The Artist' written by Mabel Cox. In it, she described him as *"the greatest living authority on dyeing and fabric printing"*. According to her, his outstanding achievement was the discovery of good mordants. (Mordants enable the dye to penetrate the cloth.) Even when he used the old vegetable dyes, the mordants were newly researched and scientifically improved. When used with the traditional Indian dyes and tans, the Indians themselves were astonished by the results. The efficacy of the mordants were reflected in the fastness of the colours. *"Most Wardle-dyed fabrics"*, wrote Mabel Cox, *"may safely go through the ordinary washtub, and even red may be boiled without injury"*.

She described how Thomas kept an exposure book for materials exposed to the sun. Vegetable dyes stood the test better than chemical ones. *"Some of the latter are found to be absolutely colourless after twelve months' exposure. This is the result of the rage for cheapness which is rampant. The material must be cheap and consequently it is made largely of rubbish to last a month or two, at the end of which time a new colour will come into fashion and the old material be no longer required. Therefore it does not matter if it is threadbare and faded into colourless streaks. Probably its owner will be all the better pleased to have an excuse to indulge in the latest fashion, assuredly a lamentable condition of public taste. Sir Thomas has shown we can all have permanent colours and beautiful fabrics if we wish..."* A harsh judgment on the followers of fashion, but an excellent advertisement for the Wardle dye works.

As a speaker, Thomas had always been in demand. He had a lively delivery, always took plenty of visual aids, and could be relied upon to provide his audience with interesting anecdotes as well as sound information. A typical example was an address he gave on 'Arts, Crafts and Industry' at the prizegiving of the School of Art in Newcastle-under-Lyme in 1898. Recalling that he had visited the School on a similar occasion in 1882 to speak about art training, Thomas said: *"I have often wondered if it did any good"*. He told the students that he had discovered that Gladstone had presented four pamphlets to the Saltney Library of Chester, one of which was a copy of his speech to them in 1882. He had bribed that Saltney Library to let him have the Gladstone copy in return for a few others and a year's subscription so he could see the great man's underlining and marginal inscriptions. (This had been picked up by the Staffordshire Sentinel.) A tick, a single line, a double line and a double line plus an 'N.B.' graded the importance of his comments. If Gladstone had found it worth while, said Thomas, the students must surely have been stimulated to increased exertions.

He went on to list the reasons for the poor performance of the British export trade (which could have been written perhaps a lifetime later) and to suggest ways that the situation could be corrected:

1. *Unwillingness to supply a cheaper range of goods or to be content with a small order initially. Manufacturers should study the wishes of the customer*
2. *They should adopt the metric system.*
3. *Commercial travellers should be able to negotiate in the customer's own language.*
4. *Inferior packing and inartistic labelling.*
5. *The extra cost of freight on British steamers.*
6. *Frequency of strikes, making delivery dates unreliable.*
7. *Poor technical education compared to that in continental countries, especially Germany.*

He concluded that it was the duty of British industrialists to remedy these faults so that today's students could keep abreast of foreign competition.

The text of another address, this time to the Architectural Association on the printing of textiles, was published in 1899. This was a particularly interesting lecture because of its references to William Morris. After showing slides to illustrate textile design from the ancient world to the Italian renaissance, Thomas went on to say *"...from 1800 we arrive at distressing decadence, artistic inspiration gives way to commonplace designers and it is not until we come to the Morrisian period of our own times that pattern designing as a worthy art has reappeared."* Design had at last started to improve, he continued, partly because of the influence of teachers in the provincial art schools who had been properly trained at South Kensington, and also through the influence of the late William Morris, *"...a very great man in any form of art. His skill was partly intuitive and partly the result of studying olden artistic work. The slightest departure from colour harmony jarred on his mind and eye like an unresolved discord on the ear. He was a perfectionist. I should have known little of printing but for him. After his success in his beautiful wall paper designing, he appealed to me to join him in an attempt at improving the art of tissue printing.....rather rashly, I undertook the task being led on by the charm of his personality and the wide range and power of his artistic ability – he insisted on a revival of old processes of printing colour, and on vegetable dyes. Together we studied Italian, French and English books of the last four centuries, and when in India I had to study the native methods of printing their designs."*

He told them that the first design for cotton cloth that Morris produced was Marigold, and was probably his best. Simplicity, beautiful drawing and harmony of colour were the hall-marks. On the Wardle table there had been a cloth of Morris' Honeysuckle design for twenty years, and they still liked it. Finally Thomas showed some slides of modern design by Walter Crane and others, adding *"I hope I may be pardoned for including a few designs by my youngest son, who has been trained to the work."* Young Tom was indeed very gifted and his designs were every bit as good as those of established artists of the modern school.

1899 saw the start of the Boer War. Elizabeth was asked by the Countess of Dartmouth to be the President of SSAFA for the Leek district. Although her health had not been good, she threw herself into the work with her customary practicality and good organising ability. *"No family should be in need because the breadwinner is called up".* She was already Honorary Secretary to the Leek branch of the North Staffordshire Needlework Guild. They already supplied clothes for the needy, especially children, so one aspect of the relief work was simple for her to cater for. SSAFA meetings were held at the Wardle home, and the Leek Post agreed to publish weekly the list of donations. Her family helped her; Bernard's wife was one of the collectors; Gilbert and his wife gave £5 to the fund, Bernard £2, Arthur £1, while Thomas and Elizabeth jointly gave £10. (Evidently Arthur felt his contribution had not been sufficient, for in the next issue he was down as having given two guineas.) There was also a scheme for supplying beef tea 'and other nourishments' to the sick. Among her friends she found volunteers who would do this for a month each, while drugs and dressings were to be paid for from a Samaritan fund. In two years she was responsible for raising £1056.11.3 for servicemen's families in the district and had organised a rota for visiting them.

Elizabeth developed a heart condition which worsened rapidly when she exerted herself in her SSAFA work (the Soldiers, Sailors and Air Force Association - it was always known as SSAFA, although the 'Air Force' reference did not come in until later.) A year or two previously, she had taken to rising early to finish some embroidery she had planned for her children. *"I want them each to have something to remember me by."* It was well that she started this project before she became ill, since by the Autumn of 1900 she was housebound and not strong enough to go on working in the early morning.

The Duke and Duchess of York came to Leek that July, for the opening of the new Technical Institute by the Duchess and the laying of the foundation stone of the William Carr Gymnasium by the Duke. The Institute was the realisation of a dream for Thomas, and one shared by Elizabeth as well, for she too had been a member of the Leek Technical Instruction Committee. The Royal party arrived mid-afternoon, accompanied by the Duke and Duchess of Sutherland. Thomas had the honour of presenting various local dignitaries, having ridden in the second carriage in the procession. His granddaughter Dorothy, Bernard's little girl, presented one of the bouquets. At the site of the gymnasium, Thomas handed over a cheque for £1000 towards the completion of the building, the result of a collection throughout the town. After the ceremonies, the royal pair were taken to the Nicholson Institute where the silk manufacturers had put on an exhibition. Tea was served in the reading room by Mrs Nicholson, widow of the donor of the building. Elizabeth was not well enough to attend the ceremonies, greatly to her disappointment, but the Duchess knew the Wardles well, from the days when her mother, the Duchess of Teck, had been president of the Ladies' Silk Association – on her mother's death, she had taken over the Presidency herself and was very active in her support for British silk (there was a Wardle family story that Thomas had been permitted to call her by her Christian name when she was a young girl). The Duchess was aware of Elizabeth's indisposition and disappointment, so after the formal tea had ended, she and the Duke paid a brief visit to 54 St.Edward Street to see 'dear Lady Wardle'. The gesture was a great source of pleasure and consolation to Elizabeth.

Thomas was engaged in preparing for yet another exhibition that autumn; the Women's Exhibition at Earls Court. The Silk Association contributed a display, but what took most of Thomas' attention were the Kashmiri silks and brocades. The results of the harvest of the new European seed had been good, and he was anxious to make full use of the opportunity to publicise it. In his book on the Kashmir silk industry, there is a photograph of the exhibit at Earls Court. There were eight double glass fronted display cabinets full of materials, shown under the name of the Maharajah. As described in the catalogue they contained:

1. Raw silk, organzine, and tram 'in gum', undyed.
2. Figured and plain brocades, damasks, etc. all manufactured from raw silk produced in Kashmir in 1898 and 1899, for Upholstery, Decorative and Dress purposes, in English, Indian, Venetian and French styles and designs. The silk dyed with pure unweighted dyes by Messrs. Joshua Wardle and Sons, Silk Dyers, Leek, Staffordshire, and woven by Messrs Warner and Sons of Braintree and Spitalfields. This most interesting case of silk of Kashmir production is illustrative of the successful attempt within the last few years to introduce sericulture into Kashmir, the climate of which is extremely favourable both for the rearing of the silk worm and cultivation of the mulberry leaves upon which feeds.

The Maharajah was fortunate to have someone experienced in exhibition work to arrange the display. But the display was only the final stage of a publicity campaign that Thomas had been waging on behalf of Kashmir's silk. He had found that manufacturers were prejudiced against it, thinking it was of the same quality as silk from Bengal. They told him, *"Oh, we know Indian silk very well; it will not suit our textiles, we have repeatedly tried it"*. He went armed with samples to most of the large silk users in England and several on the continent *"at considerable expense, trouble and anxiety to convince the manufacturers and dealers that it was not Indian silk at all, but that of the very best race of silk worms from France, grown in Kashmir from imported eggs."* Ever persuasive, Thomas managed to cajole most of them into trying it, and as a result there was a demand for Kashmir silk. It was already fetching only 1/- or 2/- less than the best Italian and French in the raw, and as soon as the reeling process was perfected there was no reason why its quality should not reach the best European standards. Without the very active Wardle support, the silk from Kashmir might not have achieved its early recognition or success.

Elizabeth's health gave her family great concern. Her eldest daughter Lydia was unmarried and still at home and she did as much as possible to lighten the load on her mother. The last major work that Elizabeth undertook in the embroidery field, was to arrange a new white altar frontal designed by John Sedding for St.Edward's Church, which was then worked by the parishioners. After that, Lydia gradually assumed the running of the School of Embroidery when Elizabeth was poorly, and took over some of her mother's public work as well. In this she was helped by her youngest sister Lizzie, who by now had married her cousin Horace (son of George) and lived in Leek near to the family home.

After much nursing and loving care, it was no surprise to her family when Elizabeth died on September 8th 1902, aged 68. She was buried in the family vault at Cheddleton, where she had lived at the beginning of her married life. The open vault was decorated by her niece Nellie and two other members of the Leek Embroidery Society. Her two favourite hymns were sung, accompanied on the harmonium because the organ was out of order. Telegrams of condolence poured in from all over the country, from an impressive list of titled persons headed by Her Royal Highness, the Princess of Wales and the Duchess of Sutherland, and by no fewer than three Bishops. But the tributes which must have meant most to the family were those from the staff at Thomas' office, the servants at Swainsley, the Leek Embroidery Society and one from Mrs Lowe, widow of Thomas' old friend Charles, who had died a couple of years previously.

A memorial leaflet was printed shortly afterwards which traced her life and achievements. According to the author, her death was caused by cardiac trouble aggrevated by asthma and indigestion. Her warm heart and generosity had endeared her to the people of Leek, also her practical approach to problems. She had never refused anyone in need. After her death, it was discovered that she had regularly been giving the profits of the Embroidery School to various charities, and in some years the gifts had actually exceeded the income and had to be financed from her own pocket. She had been a good-looking woman as well as a generous one – the leaflet described her as 'handsome in physical development' – although portly in later life (not surprisingly, after 14 children!)

Her family had loved her dearly and were desolated to lose her. But of course it was Thomas who missed her most of all. Looking back over their long life together, he must have remembered the early days of their marriage when they ran the Cheddleton Sunday School together; the lost babies; her courage during her long illness after Lizzie was born; her support for his tussur experiments and the marvellous achievements of her Leek Embroidery; the well ordered household and warm hospitality to all his many friends; her help in his Silk Association activities and exhibitions; and, latterly, the shared love they both had for Swainsley. She had outstanding gifts, but the greatest one was her warm personality which won her the lasting affection of all her family and friends.

Kashmir Silks at the Earl's Court Exhibition of 1900

The Duke & Duchess of York at the opening of the Leek Technical Schools, July 25th 1900.

HRH the Duke of York laying of the Foundation Stone, Carr Gymnasium, July 25th 1900

Margaret Elizabeth Wardle
(1869-1949), who later married
Phillip Jukes Worthington

Mrs Worthington (later Lady Gaunt), outside Stockwell House, 1903

Chapter Nine

KASHMIR

After the death of Elizabeth, Thomas continued to live at 54 St.Edward Street in Leek, spending weekends at Swainsley whenever possible. Lydia, who had not married, kept house for him and carried on the work of the Embroidery Society. His youngest daughter, Lizzie, and her husband Horace lived in Hugo Street, where he was a frequent visitor. As a memorial to Elizabeth, Thomas and the family gave a stained glass window by Morris and Co. to St.Edward's church, where it can be seen on the South wall. Dedicated to 'Dame' Elizabeth Wardle, it would nowadays be considered incorrect, but at that time it was not unusual for ladies of distinction to be known as 'Dame' as a mark of affectionate respect.

In the February after Elizabeth's death, Thomas was made an Honorary Freeman of the Worshipful Company of Weavers. This was a rare honour and one he appreciated immensely, both for its own sake but also because it opened the door for yet another; in July 1903 he became a Freeman of the City of London. Both these entitlements gave him great pleasure. The City of London scroll was framed and hung in his office, an object of much pride, and is still in the possession of his descendants.

Now in his 70s, Thomas' energy was still remarkable and his enthusiasm for silk undiminished. For the Association, there were more exhibitions, more campaigns and more travels. His recreations continued as before; shooting, fishing, music and the Field Club. The only concession he seems to have made to advancing years was to go to the South of France or Italy for a few weeks every Winter to convalesce after bronchial attacks. He had not had the money or the time for this in earlier years, but now he was able to indulge himself a bit.

The last years of his life held two main interests; Kashmir, and the Leek and Manifold Railway. The continuing story of the infant silk industry in Kashmir is recounted in Thomas' book 'Kashmir and its new Silk Industry', published in 1904. As mentioned previously, through seven years of correspondence with Mr.Walton, Thomas had directed matters from afar. There was frustration when expansion was blocked by insufficient funds and staffing, but in general he was delighted by the increasingly successful harvests from the European silk seed and by the quality of the raw silk produced. The Resident, Sir Adelbert Talbot, was equally delighted when the new industry made a profit for the State of Kashmir of over £13000 for the season 1899–1900.

But by 1903, Thomas became seriously alarmed by rumours and threats that the silk industry could be taken over by private enterprise. Mindful of what had happened in Bengal, he was convinced that the only way for the industry to develop was under state control; the private entrepreneur would make a quick profit without ploughing back anything into the concern, and he greatly feared that home-bred seed would be substituted for the disease-free European variety for the sake of economy. As always, the voices of the would-be private industrialists were loud and persuasive. There was even an official conference to discuss the matter. One of the arguments put forward to persuade the Government of Kashmir to relinquish control was that over the previous few years, the industry had actually made a loss and the Accountant General was quoted as having confirmed this.

These efforts to take the industry into private hands were strenuously opposed by Thomas, and once again he wrote to everyone he could think of who could have any influence in the matter. As he said, it was the State of Kashmir that had the foresight and courage to start the cultivation of european seed; it was the State which had financed the new filatures and paid the assistants. So it was entirely right that the profit should go back to the State coffers. He added "...I would like here to remark that the question of the employment of thousands of native Kashmiris, greatly needing occupation and being on the brink of starvation, had more weight with me than the mere profit-making..."

As for the allegation that the industry had been losing money, he could not believe it to be true, so soon after Sir Adelbert Talbot's announcement of a £13,000 profit. A new Resident had just been appointed and Thomas found great difficulty in discovering the truth of the matter. "So", he said, "I felt much alarm on the ground of my own moral responsibility in having advised the Government to commence this industry. I decided to go out to Kashmir at my own expense to see into matters for myself."

Now that Elizabeth's long struggle against ill-health was over, and his sons and son-in-law were managing the three dyeworks satisfactorily, Thomas felt free to go. He had longed to return to India, and had probably hoped for an official invitation, but that had not been forthcoming. Accordingly, he made his plans to go to Kashmir in March 1904. He wrote to Sir Arthur Godley asking for free train passes from Bombay to Kashmir and back, via Simla. He met with the accustomed red tape; his request was to be handed on to the Government of India, since the Secretary of State did not deal with such matters. Undaunted, he then enquired if there was any hope of a free railway pass from London to Marseilles, where he planned to board a P.and O. boat. To this, he received a polite refusal, signed by Horace Walpole. After a month of such refusals and delays, Thomas decided to go forthwith. He called at the India Office in person to say he was leaving the next week, even though there had been no official confirmation that he was expected in Kashmir. The official memos arising from this visit reveal confusion and a certain amount of irritation, but a telegram was in fact sent to the Government of India warning of his impending arrival and requesting the free rail passes for him.

En route, Thomas spent a week at the French sericultural centre at Cevennes inspecting the latest procedures and equipment. During the voyage to Bombay, he wrote a report on all he had seen. He did not linger on arrival at Bombay as there was an outbreak of smallpox. He went straight to the railway station and took an express train to Jammu, Kashmir's Southern 'second city'. There he had a right royal welcome. The new Resident, Mr.Colvin, met him most cordially, and told him he would be put up at the Residency. The Maharajah sent word that he was putting at Thomas' disposal a carriage and pair, and an elephant. The elephant, Thomas proudly recorded, *"was one that had attracted special attention at the Delhi Durbar, one of the finest specimens of its kind, with its head and front richly and decoratively painted."* He did make use of his elephant, for in his book there is a photograph of it kneeling in front of the house with himself and Mrs Colvin about to descend from the howdah by ladder after a ride out to the Fort.

A special Durbar was called by the Maharajah so that he and his brother could welcome Thomas and hear his views on the silk industry. He started by showing them the latest tavelettes he had seen in France, and he read the report he had written during his voyage. This was considered so important that the Maharajah ordered it to be printed immediately by the State press. Much encouraged, Thomas broached the subject of the future ownership of the silk industry. Greatly to his relief, the royal brothers were most emphatic that it should remain in State hands and not be handed over to commercial interests!

Thomas had brought out with him the very fine black figured brocades which had been woven by Warners from some of the earliest Kashmiri silk for the Earl's Court exhibition. The Durbar assembly was delighted to see these, and it was decided to offer one piece to the new Queen, Alexandra, and another to the Princess of Wales – formerly Princess May of Teck. Thomas was asked to present the brocades to the Royal ladies on his return to England, on behalf of the Maharajah. With everyone full of praise for the brocades, the opportunity came for Thomas to raise the subject which had been uppermost in his mind for many months; namely, the introduction of silk weaving in Kashmir. Now that the initial problems of reeling had been overcome, he strongly advocated this as an extension to the silk industry. In his own words, *"...the reeling of the cocoons had been brought about, under Mr.Walton's able supervision, to such perfection, that I felt sure there was now a possibility of weaving goods quite equal in texture and fineness to those so largely exported from China and Japan."* These latter were in great demand in the West because neither European nor American weavers could produce goods as cheaply. Japanese wages for silk weaving had recently risen to 6d per day, so with Kashmiri wages only 4d per day, it would be a good moment to start weaving, with excellent prospects of production at very competitive prices. Moreover, there was a vast market for woven silk near at hand in India.

Much to Thomas' delight, the Maharajah and his brother immediately approved the suggestion and promised support. The development would be a major step as there was no local tradition of weaving in Kashmir. Considerable capital investment would be needed, but there would be no shortage of labour or of raw silk. Thomas was commissioned to send out from England an experienced weaver and 200 looms for the first factory.

There was one difficulty that Thomas had not mentioned at the Durbar, and that was the yellow tinge in the local silk. For the new weaving to succeed, it must compare favourably with the Chinese and Japanese products in every respect. The silk from both countries was very white in colour, and its popularity in the West was partly due to this. If Kashmir was to weave silk that could be dyed in pale pastel shades, something had to be done to eradicate the yellow tinge. Thomas had consulted with his sons and between them a formula was produced *"so to whiten Kashmir woven silk that it can hardly be distinguished from the white silk of Japan"*. Never slow to praise his own achievement, Thomas added, *"this is a discovery of the highest importance and will make the progress of a weaving industry in Kashmir much less difficult of success and of sale"*.

Having achieved so much in the first few days of his visit in Jammu, the capital city of Srinagar was next on his itinerary, where Mr. Walton awaited him. The nearest he could get by train was Rawal Pindi, where the railway ended. The last 200 miles to Srinagar had to be covered by tonga, staying at government guest houses along the route. The journey took four days and was distinctly perilous as the snows had not yet melted. He left alone in a tonga, despite being warned that he would probably have to walk for two miles through the snow at the highest point of the pass. Horses were changed every five or six miles, for the track was rough and steep. At one point he had to leap out of the tonga to avoid a rock fall with the overhanging snows above him and the river foaming in flood a thousand feet below.

Arrived at Srinagar, he found that his accommodation this time was to be on a houseboat, complete with five servants and twelve boatmen. After all the years of correspondence, he was delighted to meet Mr Walton again in person. When he was shown the new filatures and the reelers at work, Thomas wrote, *"I have never seen a people so marvellously clever with their fingers as the Kashmiris. It is a sight to go down to the bassines in the filatures and see the beautiful way men and boys can handle the fine threads of the cocoons, even those who have been engaged in it for a few weeks only. They do it with a readiness and skill which compare favourably with the south of Europe fileuses, who have gone through an apprenticeship to learn cocoon reeling......There are 550 men and boys in each of the six filatures, with four more being built.......To think that this immense industry had all developed from the £6-£700 worth of silk worm eggs I bought six years ago seemed wonderful, and made one feel very thankful."* He went on to record the numbers of people employed in the new industry:

Silk rearers (average of 4 to a family)...............	44,600
Reelers and turners in 6 filatures......................	3,300
Sorters...	200

146

Packing and deniering...	60
Firemen and woodcutters (there was no coal)...........	50
Carting wood...	40
Additional reelers when new filature completed..........	2,200
Total:	50,450

It read like a fairy tale, said Thomas; to have over 50,000 people previously so poor they were starving, employed in an industry which had not existed six years ago. He was particularly keen that women should be recruited for the next two filatures, saying that female employment would be a great blessing and lessen the degradation of their lives.

When Thomas drove up the Vale of Kashmir, he saw that the prevailing species of mulberry tree was black, and only 5% were white. He immediately recommended that any new planting should be the white variety, which would lighten the shade of the resultant cocoons. He was also shocked to see the way the natives lopped whole branches of trees in their search for mulberry leaves to feed the silk worms. *"The trees are hacked in the most ignorant way when the sap is rising...the most valuable branches have been cut away with axes so that the leaves can be gathered from the ground. If this deplorable state of things is permitted to go on for the next 4 or 5 years there will be no mulberry leaves to gather. The use of the axe should positively be prohibited. I have never witnessed a case so illustrative of killing the goose for the sake of its golden eggs".* Thomas never minced his words; his shocked disapproval did result in the appointment of a properly trained State forestry officer, mandatory directives on pruning and a lot of new mulberry plantations.

As well as the devastated mulberry trees, Thomas found several other causes for disquiet. One was the financial aspect. He found that a proper audit had not been made for over three years. At his request, the State Accountant drew up a preliminary balance for the silk industry while he was still there. This disproved conclusively the reports of a loss which had so much worried him. Indeed, it showed an even greater profit than the figure given by Sir Adelbert Talbot without including the estimated worth of the stock of cocoons still unreeled from the previous season. Thomas was relieved that his fears had been unfounded.

Another unsatisfactory matter had been the packing of the raw silk for export. Before he left England, Thomas had received complaints from a French firm at Lyons that a large consignment of silk from Kashmir had arrived in a moth-eaten state. On inspection of the opened bales, Thomas had to agree that the silk was obviously defective, but he was not satisfied that insects were the cause. After microscopic examination, he established that the damage had been occurred in transit, through the cords being too tight and the bales rubbing against each other. The rough mountainous road from Srinagar to Rawal Pindi by pack mule was a severe test of any packaging. At least Thomas had cleared the silk from the charge of being mite infested, and while he was on the spot he was able to advise on better packing arrangements and stress the importance that there should be no re-occurrence.

At the end of his visit, Thomas had another meeting with the Durbar and made recommendations on many matters; the need for more properly trained assistants for Mr.Walton, the desirability of employing some female labour, the best way to distribute the seed to the rearers, and the immense advantage that would result from the introduction of electric power for reeling and for heating the bassines. Most of these were acted upon after his departure, through the efforts of the faithful Mr.Walton.

Since Thomas had gone at his own expense, he felt justified in spending a couple of weeks on his favourite pursuits; geology and shooting. The snow clad ranges of the Western Himalayas surround the valley of Kashmir. Thomas found the geology unfamiliar but fascinating. He took back with him to England 38 specimens of rocks and fossils, which were carefully and accurately drawn by his niece Nellie and appear in his book. (After the Field Club had seen them, they were presented to the Sedgewick Museum at Cambridge.) It says a lot for his devotion to geology that Thomas managed to collect these specimens at his age. He described his expeditions thus: *"...from the base of the mountain to a height of 9–10,000 feet part of the ascents were on pony back, but after that on foot, the ascents being too steep for pony climbing, so steep in some parts that it was difficult to hold on except by the rock stratification ledges. I got to consider an angle of 45 degrees a gentle slope. A coolie carried my hammer and specimen bag, another my shotgun, my shikari carried my rifle, and I supported myself with a stiff Alpenstock, or – rather – Himalayan stock."*

As for shooting, once again there is a long list of the animals he shot; two stags and a wild boar (the heads of which were later mounted and displayed at Swainsley), a black bear (which also ended at Swainsley, standing on its hind legs on a plinth), and 39 species of birds, the skins of which he took home with him. He used his houseboat to explore up the river, but several nights he spent in camp when game hunting – all of which he thoroughly enjoyed but it must have been quite arduous for a man of 72!

By the time he arrived back in Leek, he had been away for three and half months, the longest period he had ever been away from home. True to form, one of the first things he did was to invite the Field Club to Swainsley to see all his trophies from Kashmir. Tea was served by Lydia, who had joined the Club that year. Thomas gave a very technical address on the geology of Kashmir and displayed his collection of rocks and fossils. The other aspects of his travels had been covered by two long articles to the Leek Post which he had sent back by post, so presumably the members were well informed about his other activities.

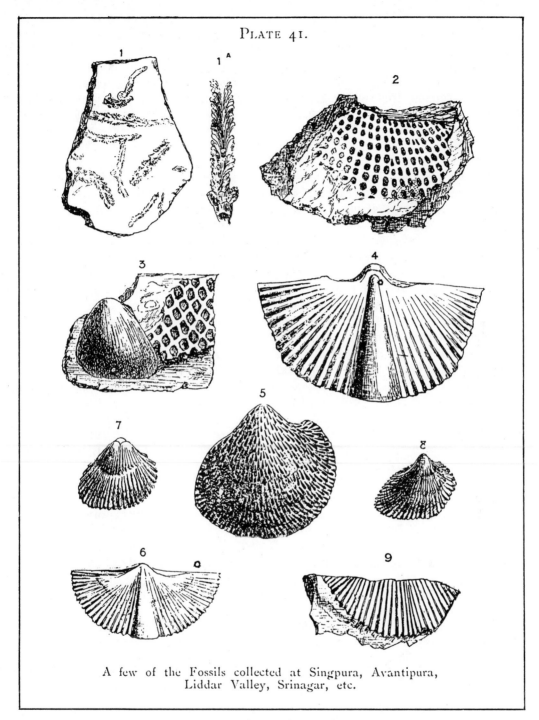

PLATE 41.

A few of the Fossils collected at Singpura, Avantipura, Liddar Valley, Srinagar, etc.

Reproduced from Thomas Wardle's
KASHMIR: its new silk industry, natural history, geology, sport etc. (1904)

Once home, Thomas lost no time in starting preparations for the projected weaving industry for Kashmir. With his friend Kershaw, from Macclesfield, he drew up plans for a hand loom factory capable of accomodating 100-200 looms. ("...the consideration of power looms must be left to the future.") He also arranged for twelve craftsmen to be sent out to Kashmir with an experienced weaver. An assistant for Mr. Walton was selected, who was to receive a six month 'crash course' in the filatures in France en route for the East.

During the Autumn, Thomas wrote a detailed report for the India Office. He ended it with an assessment of his achievements in Kashmir: *"As my life is drawing to its close, I am, I hope, not unnaturally desirous of putting on record some statement of my life work for India.....To me, it has been indeed a labour of love, which has increased with years and still continues. I have never had any desire to work for the silk interests of India from pecuniary motives, and, although the time spent is enormous, and the hobby a costly one, I have no regrets. On the contrary, I cherish a pride in my efforts, I hope justified by their success.....an historical industry which had been allowed to die out.....and employed only a few hands in 1896-7, now gives employment to more than 50,000 men women and children, all natives of the country, the rearers nearly all working in their own homes in the villages of the Valley of Kashmir and the reelers working in the filatures at Srinegar, the only Europeans engaged in this colossal industry being the Directing Superintendant and his five assistants".*

This sounded valedictory, but was far from being the end of his correspondence with the India Office. The Maharajah's request that Thomas should present the black Kashmiri brocades to the Queen and the Princess of Wales caused a flurry of letters. His baggage took months to follow him to England, and it was not until February 1904 that the presentations could be made. The India Office obviously did not appreciate the finer points because the two lengths of brocade were thought to be identical and were described as 'shawls'. Thomas wrote immediately: *"I can tell which is meant for the Queen when I see them"*, and requested ornamental boxes to put them in.

The Princess of Wales was available straightaway, and the little ceremony took place in the drawing room at Marlborough House. It was not so easy to arrange to see the Queen. First she was in Denmark, then in Ireland – and then Thomas went to the South of France to convalesce after his annual bronchitis. In the meantime, the Maharajah's brother wrote to enquire if the brocades had been presented as they were wondering why they had not heard from the Royal ladies. Three times, Thomas gave the Private Secretary at Buckingham Palace the dates when he would be in London. Finally he wrote: *"I waited in London last week expecting a summons from the Palace, but now I have returned home. I am beginning to think it might be more advisable if the presentation were made from the India Office to prevent more delay.....No doubt the Maharajah is anxious to hear about the brocade being offered and received. My part in the matter need be of no account. I do not expect to be in London again for a month."* A soothing letter came immediately, and finally a date in June was arranged. The presentation was not without drama for Thomas; his train broke down at Willesden and arrived half an hour late. He had barely time to go to his Club to collect the brocade and arrived at Buckingham Palace with only three minutes to spare. He reported that the Queen appeared delighted with the silk material, and also graciously accepted some Kashmiri needlework he offered her.

Later in 1904, Thomas was saddened to hear of the death from Bright's disease of Mr.Walton while back in this country on sick leave. He at once telegraphed the India Office, requesting that the Resident be told and asked to break the news to Walton's wife and daughters. Incredibly, this caused a flurry of internal memos about the irregularity of sending such a telegram at Government expense: *"...not usual to telegraph out the death even of an officer of the Government of India, and Mr Walton was not that, being under the Government of Kashmir. But it seems undesirable to refuse Sir Thomas Wardle's request..."* Thomas had prevailed over officialdom in this small matter, but was not so successful when he went personally to the India Office with a letter pleading the case for a compassionate grant for Mrs Walton.

This death was a severe blow to the Kashmir silk industry, especially when the weaving development was still in its infancy. However, the assistants, including the new man who had been sent for six months' training in France, were well trained and carried on where Mr.Walton had left off. The new weavers had made a good start. Only one yard a day was produced to begin with but after two months the output went up to four, and then to seven yards a day. Plain silk was all they could tackle at first, but they soon progressed to patterns, and it was not long before the Kashmir silks were really competitive with Chinese and Japanese products. By 1905, Thomas was able to tell the India Office in his annual report that the crop had nearly doubled since the previous year. He had sent 200 looms out to Srinagar, and was delighted that some of the earliest woven silk had been bought by Liberty's at a higher price than thay would have paid for Japanese silk. Also, the Continental throwsters had already announced their preference for the raw silk from Kashmir. The replies from the India Office were very different these days. Sir Arthur Godley wrote on several occasions of their recognition of *"...the continued and successful efforts which you are making on behalf of the industry in Kashmir"*.

In April 1904, Thomas made his final will. The bronchial attack he suffered that Spring may have helped to make him decide to do this. But several recent developments in the family also meant that he wanted to make specific provisions for his children. For instance, Margaret's husband, Philip Worthington, had died, leaving her a widow with a young son to support. Gilbert, Arthur and Tom each had a thousand pound loan from their father outstanding, and Bernard had borrowed a considerable sum for the Hencroft works from Parr's Bank, for which Thomas was the guarantor. The will was a long and complicated document, for Thomas provided against every eventuality, even to laying down which bookseller his library should be sold to (Quaritch, or Batsford). It began simply enough, with legacies of £100 to each of George's four unmarried daughters, to each of his grandchildren when they reached the age of twenty-one, and to William Young, a cousin of Elizabeth. (Lydia's second name was Young, presumably after the same side of the family.)

The Churnet works of Joshua Wardle and Co. were not his to dispose of, but he had bought the Hencroft works himself and he directed that they should be sold on his death, but that Tom should have the first option of purchasing the works with Bernard being offered the option if Tom did not take it up. Various provisions were made for the loans to be subtracted from the eventual shares which the sons received, except for Arthur, who had half his loan remitted. Relationships within the family can only be guessed, but it would seem that Arthur was the son to whom Thomas was most protective and Bernard was the one who incurred his father's displeasure. The will made it plain that Thomas was worried about Tom's future, as he made provision for his youngest son's continued employment by saying that he should be taken into partnership at either the Churnet or the Leekbrook works should he not be able to continue at Hencroft.

The daughters were to have generous settlements, except for Lizzie who was not mentioned, presumably because her husband, Horace, was one of the partners at the Churnet Works and therefore she would be amply provided for. Within two years, the terms of the will were varied by two codicils: one related to Margaret, who had remarried and her inheritance was brought into line with those of her sisters; the other, dated July 1906, altered the previous provisions for Tom, who had left the Hencroft Works and repaid the loan from his father. There is no record of why Tom left Leek. Maybe he was tired of working with his brother Bernard and wanted to strike out on his own. He went to the South of England, married a French lady called Gabrielle and had four children. His early promise as a textile designer, however, does not seem to have blossomed any further.

In no way did the will-making detract from Thomas' zest for life. All the old interests remained. He was still a regular attender at the meetings of the Society for the Protection of Ancient Buildings. He entered into a fierce argument over the installation of the new organ in Lichfield Cathedral. He considered the necessary alterations would be detrimental to the fabric, but it was an argument he lost. A couple of years later, the Leek council was proposing to pull down the old almshouses and Thomas went into battle again to try to save them. He rightly said that they could be modernised and there was no need to demolish the ancient and picturesque buildings which were so much a part of old Leek. Many agreed with him, but his intemperate language on the subject and his public disparagement of the Leek councillors' ability and artistic appreciation were embarrassing to his supporters.

Thomas used to meet his brother-in-law, George Y. Wardle, at these meetings, but for the last few years of his life George retired to a nursing home in Margate and remained very much of an invalid until he died in 1910. Other members of the council of the S.P.A.B. had become firm friends of Thomas, notably Bishop Stubbs of Truro. When the Bishop wrote the words for a new carol, 'Christ was born on Christmas night', Thomas set it to music, and the Embroidery Society made a beautiful presentation cover for the music in shot silk with gold on white Leek work. Thomas had arranged a good deal of church music over the years; besides the music for Margaret's wedding, he had composed a setting of the Kyrie and other chants, and also had two drawing room pieces to his credit, 'The Colonel's Leave' and 'Fishing Song'. Doubtless the favourable reception of his music emboldened him to offer to set the Bishop's carol to music.

Among his geological friends was the Curator of the Jermyn Street Museum of Practical Geology, J.Allen Howe. Walking together on the moors near Butterton, Thomas found a fossil fern on a bed of black shale which greatly excited the two friends. It did not seem to conform with any known fossil, and with high hopes that it would prove to be a new species the specimen was sent to three different, experts, including Thomas' friend Dr.Smith Woodward of the Geological Department of the British Museum *("...his father was my schoolfellow at Macclesfield sixty years ago.")*. The Sedgewick Museum at Cambridge examined it and suggested the fossil was of the Adianthus family, probably of the Species Antiquus. Thomas disputed these opinions and showed slides to the Field Club to support his belief that the fern was indeed a new species. He owned that *"the wish was father to the thought, and awakens old temptations to honour our own neighbourhood with a new species."* The argument was won by Thomas' enthusiasm and persuasion: the fossil fern was finally named 'Adiantites Wardlei'. This was the highlight of his geological career and he was enormously proud to have a species attributed to the Wardle name. Later that year, when members of the British Fern Society visited his garden at Swainsley and greatly admired his fernery, he told them the fossil fern gave him more pride and pleasure than the live specimens they had come to see.

Ever since his early days with the Field Club, Thomas had advocated the establishment of a fossil collection in the town of Leek. He had argued that it would be an invaluable source of instruction for the school children, and would increase the pride and interest of adults in their own countryside. He now decided to give his own collection to the Nicholson Institute. There were nearly 300 carboniferous limestone fossils in the collection which were carefully labelled, listed and arranged on shelves in a cabinet in the Institute. He followed up the gift by a comprehensive list of possible specimens so that future budding geologists would know what was needed to make the collection complete and to encourage them to add to it.

He could justly be proud of the collection, product of fifty years' work in the field, but it must have been sad to let them at last out of his own possession. It is a good thing that he never knew the ultimate fate of his geological treasures. In 1960, the Nicholson Institute decided to make an Arts Club room and needed more space. The collection was therefore split up between two schools, the Waterhouses Secondary School and the Leek High School. Some remnants may still be used for teaching purposes but the majority seem to have lost their labels, and been reduced to practically nothing, including the precious Adiantites Wardlei!

ADIANTITES WARDLEI, Howe

Mrs Colvin and Thomas Wardle at the Residency, Jammu,
returned from an elephant ride to the Fort.

Mr Colvin, the Resident, General Raja Sit Amar Singh and Thomas Wardle

One of the two State Elephants of H H the Maharaja Sahib of Jammu and Kashmir,
as caparisoned for the Delhi Durbar of 1902

Srinagar Silk Filature. Length 435', Width 42'. Containing 550 workers

Interior of
Filature in
operation

Baleing Room
of the
Srinagar Silk
Filature

'Souvenirs of Sport' shot in the Himalayas by Thomas Wardle during his 1903 visit to Kashmir. Also pictured are a selection of curios collected during that journey.

Chapter Ten

THE RAILWAY AND THE TERMINUS

Throughout his life, Thomas had been involved in a succession of battles, but the one that clouded his last years concerned the Leek and Manifold Valley Light Railway. It affected his dyeworks, caused trouble between him and his brother George, and threatened the beauty of his beloved Swainsley.

Before 1896, the promotion of any new railway had needed an Act of Parliament. But that year the Light Railways Act was passed, and thereafter Commissioners were set up to examine applications for light railways, with powers to award an order to proceed. This relaxation of the regulations resulted in many new schemes, including one from Leek.

It was the Vicar of Leek who had first suggested a railway to link the town with the Manifold Valley, as early as November 1895, when the new Act was still only under discussion. The main reasons for considering such a development were, firstly, to help the farmers with transport for their dairy products, and, secondly, to open up the beautiful but very remote valley for tourism. As soon as the Act had been passed, the first public meeting was called in Leek to discuss the matter. Colonel Bill, the local Member of Parliament, agreed to chair a steering committee and there seemed to be sufficient support for the project to go ahead.

Within six months, several decisions had been made: The line was to stretch from Waterhouses to Hulme End, a distance of 8 miles 8 chains; there were to be nine stations en route, but no turntables; and it was to be narrow gauge, 2ft 6ins wide. To join Leek with the head of the little railway, it was proposed to seek the support of the existing North Staffordshire Railway, which would apply under the same order for permission to construct a link line, this to be of normal gauge, 4ft 8½ins in width. It was to be completed in five years. The capital was to consist of £15,000 in £1 shares, with grants of £10,000 from both the Treasury and the Staffordshire County Council. There were to be nine directors, one of whom was to be Thomas. The lion's share of the profits was to go to the North Staffordshire Railway, for they would have responsibility for running the service.

The joint application was submitted to the Light Railway Commission in May 1897; a draft order was sent to the Board of Trade in 1898, but the final permission to proceed was not given till March 1899. Such slow progress was not to anyone's taste, least of all to Thomas. But many plans had to be made, so the time was not wasted. The consultant engineer had to be appointed and a prospectus had to be drawn up. The Company Secretary was to be Edward Challinor, a Leek solicitor whose family had been on very friendly terms for many years with the Wardles. From the outset, Challinor consulted his childhood friend, Fred Wardle, whenever he wanted a second opinion.

159

Thomas had always been in favour of progress, and could have been expected to be a natural supporter of the new scheme. However, he was ambivalent from the very start. The proposed Light Railway was to go through some of his land, and pass very near to Swainsley. He wrote to Challinor: *"Some people may like railways, I hate them. Especially when my main object in going to Swainsley was to escape railways and their noise and steam, for restfulness and undisturbedness."* (sic)

In spite of his misgivings, he was a very active director. He took on responsibility for preparing the prospectus and wrote to many of his personal acquaintances to recommend investment in the new company; he designed the seal; he headed delegations to meet with officers of the North Staffordshire Railway and he chaired meetings when Col. Bill was unable to be present. One reason for the regularity of his involvement was his determination that the railway should be tunnelled as it skirted Swainsley. As the main landowner to be affected by the new line, he felt in a sufficiently strong position to insist on this, even though it was to prove rather more costly than the alternative of a long riverside embankment and cutting.

In January 1899, before discussion on the tunnel issue had got very far, Challinor received a letter at the third Board meeting, at which Thomas was not present. It was from one of the other directors, threatening to withdraw all support because of the additional expense that a tunnel would entail. Worried, he wrote to Fred Wardle in Wakefield asking him for advice. Fred replied that his father was the only person to be so much affected by the railway, that he had made concessions over various other pieces of land required for the project, and that in his view, the Company should be pleased to have the Wardle support and not expect any further sacrifice. He also warned Challinor not to tell Thomas the name of the objector nor the personal nature of the protest. The last piece of this advice was disregarded. The fourth Board meeting was imminent and presumably Challinor felt he, must tell Thomas about the protest before he read about it in the minutes.

Thomas was furious. He wrote to Challinor: *"I was so disgusted with the selfish and ungentlemanly proposition that some influential person (or firm) would not subscribe to the Railway unless I would consent to forego a tunnel, that it has very much altered my views about the railway. If anyone thinks I am going to be bullied.....they very much mistake me. I don't care a straw whether he (or they) subscribe or not, but to lay down a provision that one must have one's quiet little place opened out for a railway in sight on at least three sides of the house is so unreasonable that I have made up my mind that I will on no account give up the tunnel and I would rather retire from the Board. I do not see, after the concessions I have made, that I ought now to be threatened about it.....The matter had been definitely settled and ought not to have been brought up again unless by myself. Kindly withdraw my name from the Board and my application for shares."*

Considering the heat of this letter, someone must have worked hard to conciliate Thomas, whether it was Challinor or a member of his family. Elizabeth was still alive and active in 1899, so she may well have had a calming influence over the matter. At any rate, the very next day he was present at the Board Meeting and there was no mention of him pulling out.

From then until the end of the year, there were constant discussions about the tunnel; the exact route it should take, the length, the height and the approaches. The consultant engineer produced four alternative schemes, two of which Thomas pronounced to be acceptable to him. On at least two occasions, Thomas took his solicitor and a land agent to Board meetings, so that his views could be professionally presented. Poor Challinor must have been heartily sick of the tunnel by the time the final decision was taken that September, for his diary of engagements on railway business shows almost daily meetings with either Thomas or his solicitor throughout June, July and August. His fellow directors were doubtless becoming exasperated as well; certainly the normally mild and restrained Colonel Bill did observe in a letter to Challinor: *"...what a fuss he is making over a small matter – he might be asking to make a light railway under Windsor Castle..."*

When the tunnel issue had been settled, Thomas found another cause for annoyance. The major operator of the enterprise, the North Staffordshire Railway, called upon the directors of the Leek and Manifold Valley Company for a joint and several guarantee and to sign a deed of personal responsibility should the money for the contract not be forthcoming. Quite rightly, Thomas insisted that this should have been made clear from the start. What was more he said, *"We are asked not only to be personally liable but also our heirs and assigns"*. An uproar of indignation broke out among the directors until Colonel Bill declared he was prepared to give an unlimited guarantee himself. This seemed to Thomas grossly unfair and immediately, without giving it much thought, he offered to share the risk with the Chairman. After the meeting he was dissuaded by Challinor from such precipitate action. Instead, he consulted with his son Fred and some of the other directors. His final decision, in line with most of the others but more generous than some, was to limit his liability to £250, and to refuse to allow it to be passed on to his heirs. This decision was a disappointment to Colonel Bill, who wrote to Challinor: *"I was rather annoyed at receiving the enclosed from Sir Thomas Wardle. It is too bad he should run in like this after the whole thing is settled, and he ought not to have done so."* It was nevertheless a wise decision, for when Colonel Bill died in 1915, the Company's overdraft caused £6500 to be paid from his estate, under the terms of his personal guarantee.

The most serious upset, however, concerned the pollution of the waters on which the Leekbrook works depended. The railway contractors, Hutchinson's, needed to purchase some land at the top of Sheephouse meadow, which formed part of the land left in trust by Joshua. The trustees were Edwin Heaton, a land surveyor from Endon, and William Allen, a solicitor from Leek. The terms of the will regarding Sheephouse read as follows:

> *"I direct that in case of any sale exchange or partition of my estate called Sheep House or any portion thereof my trustees shall make such restrictions and provisions with the purchaser or grantee thereof as will prevent abstraction from or polluting of the waters of the stream called Leek Brook flowing through such estate, so that such stream may flow uninterruptedly as at present and no damage may result to the dyeworks...it being my wish that the water of the said stream may be retained in as pure a state as practicable and without diminution."*

The will went on to direct that if any part of Sheephouse Farm was to be sold, first Thomas and then his brother George were to have the right to buy it; also that any profit deriving from such a sale should be divided between Joshua's two surviving daughters, Elizabeth Illsley (whose husband was the landlord at the Travellers' Rest nearby) and Ann, who was unmarried.

The trustees entered into negotiations with the railway company for the sale of the required land, without apparently making the required stipulations about preserving the flow and purity of the Leek Brook. No-one had foreseen how badly the brook and the wells would be affected by the construction work, but the trustees had been negligent not to provide against such an event. What was even worse, they had allowed Hutchinson's onto the land before the agreement had been settled. They were obviously reluctant to offer Thomas and George their pre-emptive rights, probably because they thought the railway would pay a better price.

All this was going on at the time of Elizabeth's death, so perhaps it was not surprising that Thomas left the matter to be dealt with by Allen and Heaton. But when he realised the extent of the damage to the water supply, he was extremely angry with the trustees, with George for not having intervened, and to a lesser extent with the two younger men Gilbert and Horace. George had retired from the works, but he still lived nearby and could reasonably have been expected to know what was happening.

Thomas described the state of the water course to the trustees thus:
> *"...the state of the water in the brook is positively frightful. It has been absolutely impossible to use it at all for any purpose now for weeks, and if it had not been for the fact of our being rather slack, as is usual at this season of the year, we should have had to make very heavy claims against Hutchinson and Co., and, as it is, we have been really very forebearing.*
> *They, on the other hand, have been exceedingly slow in bringing fresh water to the place, but I am hoping this will soon be accomplished, the pipes having recently arrived, and are being put in.*
> *I should like you to have a look at the water some time when you are passing. It is more like a sludge pool than a flood water.*
> *This is a matter of gravest importance to the future of the works, and if we can never look forward to clean water from the brooks, we shall*

have entailed upon us very heavy working expenses, in coal and steam power, in pulling the spring water across the meadows."

Joshua Wardle and Co. claimed for damages from Hutchinson's. Thomas gave Gilbert and Fred power of attorney to deal with the matter while he was away in Kashmir. On his return, he found they had assessed the damage to the business at £1000. He lost no time in increasing the claim: *"This is only an expression showing the inexperience of young men and I object to any such arrangement as accepting an equivalent sum to a supposed cost, even at the risk of a dissolution of partnership."* These were strong words, and probably Gilbert and Fred found them mortifying, but the condition of the brook was reason enough for Thomas' attitude. Since the Sheephouse land had been broached, Thomas informed the trustees, Allen and Heaton, that he wished to buy the rest of it, the parts that were not required by the railway company. They, in turn, did not intend to offer it to him until it was certain that no more would be required by Hutchinson's. There followed a prolonged wrangle between Thomas and his father's trustees which did finally result in him acquiring the land, although he had protested strongly about the price they had asked for it. Since the profit was to go to his sisters, according to the terms of the will, his reluctance to pay the assessment price did not endear him to them. George had been asked if he had any interest in acquiring the Sheephouse land and had refused. So it was left to Thomas to secure the rest of the land and water rights in the hopes that no similar damage to the purity of the water would occur again. Although his primary interest had been to safeguard the dyeworks and any personal gain to himself was negligible, the relationship between Thomas and his brother was never really repaired.

The firm of Hutchinson's also caused Thomas' wrath in relation to the construction of the narrow guage parts of the line; he grumbled about the way they used stone from Ecton quarry; he complained bitterly about the inadequate topsoil they used to cover the embankments and slopes; he encouraged and advised one of his tenants, Solomon Trueman, to claim compensation for damage and trespass on his land. Finally, the spoil heaps behind Swainsley were most unsightly. He was quite justified over these points as the contractors were not conforming to specifications, but they were for the most part working against time. The work had been delayed by an outbreak of smallpox in the labourers' huts at Butterton, while the difficult access had proved more of a hindrance than expected. His fellow directors were irritated by his critical attitude, also by his reluctance to pay for the shares he had undertaken to buy. Nevertheless, he was re-elected to the Board when his term of service expired, both in 1905 and again in 1908.

The Leek and Manifold Light Railway was opened by the Earl of Dartmouth on June 27th 1904, just under five years after the first sod had been ceremonially cut by the Duke of Devonshire at Waterhouses in October 1899. There had been a delay in testing the engines, otherwise the line would have been opened a month earlier. Thomas had offered to provide lunch at Swainsley for the great occasion, but this had been politely refused by Colonel Bill on the grounds that the house would not have been large enough, and a marquee would be more practical. The Wardle family attended in strength. Unfortunately, the North Staffordshire Railway had not finished the normal gauge part of the line. Steam buses, coke-fired to avoid a smoke problem, had to be used to take passengers from Leek to Waterhouses, a journey which took one hour and cost 8p. It was not until July 1905 that the whole line was completed and the steam buses could be dispensed with. They ended their days as removal vans.

Now that the actual construction was complete, the agenda of the Board meetings was rather different. Thomas was still an assiduous attender, often involving himself with his habitual fervour. One of these minor matters was the introduction of a post-box on the train, and another was the charge for transporting goods. Regarding the former, it was probably Thomas himself who pressed for the post-box. Negotiations between the Post Office at Leek and the North Staffordshire Railway were very protracted; when the long awaited mail box was installed on the train, Thomas was aggrieved to discover that it only operated on weekdays and not on Sundays. Writing to the railway's director in Stoke to say there must have been some mistake, a very curt reply arrived: *"If there is any mistake in the use of the letter box on Sundays, it is in your part..."* As for his second complaint, about the charge for carrying parcels on the little train, it was reported to Colonel Bill by the secretary with the comment that it was really only Thomas who was affected, and, *"frankly, I do not see why Sir should not pay..."*

But the main subject to concern all the directors was the financial situation. The line never made a profit, while the construction costs of over £52,000 were more than anticipated. The share capital was increased from the original £15,000 to £20,000; the Treasury was persuaded to increase its grant and to provide a loan of £7,500 at 3% interest, while the County Council was prevailed upon to lend £10,000 at 3½%. Even so, there was a deficit of about £15,000. The minutes of the Directors' meetings show that Thomas was constantly pressing for more frequent accounts to be shown, and for shareholders' meetings, but he received very little satisfaction.

Finally, by July 1908, Thomas could bear the situation no longer. He went above the Chairman's head and arranged a meeting at the Treasury to discuss the railway's liquidity problems. Colonel Bill was clearly put out by this. He wrote to the Secretary *"...I hear Sir Thomas Wardle has arranged to meet officials at the Treasury on Tuesday next.....he has asked me to attend, which I shall not do, but I have no objection to you giving him any information he needs. He hopes to persuade the Treasury to convert the loan into a free gift and ask for an additional grant so that Government money will be half the total cost of construction. All to the good, if he can do it."* It was not the first time that Thomas had been to the Treasury on behalf of the railway, for he had accompanied Colonel Bill in 1906, but this time it was entirely at his own initiative. He evidently did not report back to the directors on the outcome of this meeting, because by October the Secretary reported that *"Sir Thomas was far from well, confined to his bed so will not be attending a meeting for some time."* In fact, Thomas did not appear again in the minutes. He died the following January and the railway company were obliged to write to St. Edward Street to discover what the outcome of the interview had been. His pocket-book was found, in which he had written down what he had said – as was his custom – but it did not reveal what the Treasury reaction had been to Thomas' appeal. Whether his visit was the deciding factor or not, in 1909 the official decision was to suspend interest repayment for six months while the company was in difficulty, on condition that the County Council did the same. A concession, certainly, but not as helpful as Thomas would have liked.

The six month suspension of interest on the loan finally stretched out to five years. A new debenture stock of £12,000 was floated in 1911, but the debts were still crippling until Colonel Bill died in 1915. As has already been said, his personal guarantee was invoked and the overdraft was paid off from his estate. In the 1920's, the creamery at Ecton kept the railway viable, but by 1934, the situation looked more hopeless than ever and the little railway closed.

During these last years, although his predominant involvement may have been the railway, Thomas' other activities continued. His fluency in French was one of the reasons why he was chosen to represent the Macclesfield Chamber of Commerce at an international conference in Liège, and the Leek Spun Silk Company on a fact-finding tour of Switzerland. His knowledge of statistics must have been helpful when he was asked to write yet another official report, this time for the Tariff Commission.

One result of all his battles over the railway seems to have been an increasing closeness to his son Fred. Although he was the only son not to be working in Leek, Fred still kept up with his old friends and was the only one to share his father's interest in the railway. He was often consulted over other matters as well, and Thomas evidently had confidence in Fred's advice. After spending the early part of his working life in Yorkshire, Fred took a practice in Bath and moved his increasing family down there. (He finally had four sons, one of whom followed him into the legal profession). He spent several years as Town Clerk, a position he had formerly held in Bradford, before taking up private practice.

By 1907, Thomas was not doing much public speaking, but Fred managed to persuade him to speak at the annual prize giving of the Technical College and Secondary School in Bath.

The Wardle skill and charm had not abated. Thomas spoke of native dyers in Peshawar, quoted his early work with William Morris, brought in Burne-Jones with his stained glass windows and recalled conversations he had held with the Prince of Wales about colour and design. He went on to praise the syllabus of the Bath Technical College, especially giving credit for the excellent teaching of French and German; he encouraged the students to aim at university education, mentioning his work on the Cambridge University Appointments Board; finally, he talked of his annual visit to the South Kensington School of Art to see the students' work. The Bath students were impressed, as well they might be, for Thomas was a very accomplished public speaker with a wealth of experience to quote from, and for Fred's sake he was anxious to be especially interesting and inspiring. There is no record that he made any more speeches after this.

After Thomas' death, friends said his energy had deserted him during his last six months. Nevertheless, he managed to do a great deal in his final year of 1908. He had yet another honour bestowed on him that year when he was appointed Honorary Expert Referee on Silk for the Imperial Institute. He had a special brief to report on Nigerian and Ugandan silks. The Ugandan silk worm makes a silken nest for its cocoon, and Thomas pronounced it to be suitable for 'waste' use i.e. spun silk. In Nigeria, the silk is combined with cotton for native cloth, which could have had interesting applications in the British market.

There was another exhibition this year at which the Silk Association could display their wares. The last one had been in 1902, organised by Liberty's, and Thomas had had very little to do with it. But in 1908 the Franco-British Exhibition was a very much more ambitious affair, giving an opportunity for British silks to be seen side by side with their French rivals. It was held at Shepherd's Bush, and Thomas was appointed Vice-Chairman of the Jurors of the Silk Section. Exhibition work is extremely tiring, but there is no record of how far Thomas was able to carry out his duties.

The early months of the year had been clouded by the decision of Bernard to leave the Hencroft works and set up his own business at New Mills, near Stockport. He took with him the rollers, printing blocks and all the Wardle and Morris pattern books. No-one now knows the reason for Bernard's departure. Tom had left the firm two years previously, so it could not have been brotherly rivalry that was the cause. Possibly the Hencroft works had become too small for expansion to be possible – they were only 8140 square yards, and from the first, the water supply had not been of the purest quality. Maybe Thomas had interfered too much and Bernard preferred to be independent. There was also a possibility that Bernard's wife had something to do with it, for her family came from the Lancashire textile scene, and she had some money of her own. But whatever the reason, Thomas was very angry. He added another codicil to his will in October, directing that from Bernard's share of his estate deductions must be made for "...*the whole of the loss I have sustained or shall sustain by his removal of the printing business and machinery from the Hencroft works...; loss of rent while the premises remain vacant, deterioration of machinery through non-use, value of rollers, blocks and effects improperly removed from the works contrary to arrangement..."* After his death, Bernard arranged for all the pattern books to be deposited at the Whitworth Gallery in Manchester, where they still are.

Also in 1908, Thomas produced his last booklet on the divisibility of silk fibre. It was a highly technical work dealing with imperfections of silk thread. It contained the results of a piece of Italian research which supported his findings, translated into English by Thomas himself together with Miss Kate Milner of Leek, also drawings of African cocoons by his niece Elinor Wardle. Since 1901, Thomas said he had investigated the problem of specks in silk, (the Italians call it 'fiocchetti', the Americans call it 'lousiness'), and he wished to put on record his findings and advice. He probably actually wrote the text during the Winter, but the book did not appear till late Spring 1908. It certainly was not the sort of work one would expect from an elderly gentleman whose powers were failing.

It so happened that several long-term projects with which Thomas had been involved came to fruition during his last year. Firstly, he had been on the planning committee for some new galleries at the Whitworth Institute, and had even chosen the colour for the decorations. He was present in July at the opening, and approved greatly of the new additions.

Secondly, a somewhat similar occasion was the opening of the new museum in Hanley. Seven members of the North Staffordshire Field Club had combined with seven members of the Hanley Corporation to plan the building. Only six founder members of the Field Club still remained, two of whom were Thomas and William Brough. It was not surprising that they were chosen to form part of the Club's representatives on the planning committee. The opening was performed in October by Sir Oliver Lodge, Principal of Birmingham University. The two old colleagues were both on the platform for the occasion, justly proud of the new museum which promised to be a much needed centre of education and culture in North Staffordshire. It had been an enterprise greatly to Thomas' taste, giving him a chance to put into practise much of what he had been preaching for many years.

But the project nearest to Thomas' heart was the planning of a chancel and organ at the church at Warslow. The family had worshipped there when they were at Swainsley at weekends, until the little chapel at Ecton was built. Thomas had played the organ and sometimes had trained the choir, small though it was. It was decided that the rectangular building should be enhanced by adding a chancel, but such an extension would have been very costly for the sparse congregation. Thomas offered to pay for the major part of the work, and took a great interest in the planning and construction. By March, he must have felt himself to be failing for he made another codicil to his will, directing that any deficit in the cost of the alterations to Warslow Church should be paid from his estate should he not survive until the work was completed. In actual fact, he did live to see the finished chancel. He not only attended the re-opening service but also played the organ for the occasion, using some of his own settings for the hymns. Later, an East window by Morris and Co. was given by his children in memory of both their parents – the dedication is clearly inscribed. The Leek Embroidery Society made a complete set of furnishings in each of the four liturgical colours which are beautifully preserved and still in use today.

Thomas did manage a few days shooting that Autumn, but Gilbert said he tired easily. Only twelve months previously, Thomas had been fit enough to travel as far as Sugnall by train for a day's shooting, where he had been invited by the son of his old friend, Charles Lowe. The contrast must have depressed him, but he maintained his intellectual vigour till the end. In November, only two months before his death, he was writing to the Leek Post on unemployment and the harmful effects of Free Trade. Based on his correspondence with the American Silk Association, he urged a return to protectionism if the remnants of the English silk industry were to be saved.

Thomas died on the third of January 1909, surrounded by his family. In spite of a couple of months confined to the house and increasing debility, he had not been in bed until after Christmas and the end came rapidly after that. In another ten days he would have been 78.

The funeral was at Cheddleton Church, where he joined Elizabeth and so many of their children in the family vault. Not surprisingly, it was a large funeral. The cortege left from St.Edward Street and arrived at Cheddleton at 11.30a.m. The pall bearers included Sir Adelbert Talbot, Sir George Birdwood and William Brough. Psalm 90 was sung to a Wardle setting, and the flowers in church and in the vault had been arranged by the Leek Embroidery ladies. His five sons and their wives were there, but only three daughters, no mention being made of Lydia. Two of his grandsons attended, Mr Lance Worthington and Master Jack Wardle (sons of Margaret and Gilbert respectively).

Letters of condolence poured in – the one from the Princess of Wales would have given him much pleasure could he have known about it. Obituaries appeared in the journals of every society to which he had belonged, and in both national and local press. The least expected one perhaps was a memorial piece in the Field, describing him as a great

"Man goeth forth to his work, and to his labour, until the evening"

†

In Memoriam

Thomas Wardle
(of Leek)

Who died January 3rd 1909

In his 78th year

Laid to Rest
in Cheddleton Churchyard

✠

"Thou Lord art merciful, for Thou rewardest every man according to his work."

Art & Book Co. Ltd, Westminster   1305

sportsman. The most interesting was an account of his father's life by Gilbert in the Journal of Indian Arts and Crafts, most beautifully illustrated by coloured photographs of various Wardle designs for printed fabrics.

The story of Thomas' life was one of ever increasing battles, most of which he won. In business he was hard, like most Victorians, but his personal acquaintances all spoke of his genial manner, his charm and his interest in other people. He certainly kept up with his old friends, and was a most generous host both in Leek and at Swainsley. If the yardstick of success is lasting achievement, Thomas did not come out very well. His most impressive achievements in the field of silk did not survive very long. He fought long and hard against the decline of the industry, but 'artificial' silk was just around the corner and man-made materials were to follow. The Silk Association he had set up could not prevail against the flood of new invention and the change in consumer demand. He was nevertheless a remarkable man, in energy, imagination and persistence – a man of whom the town of Leek could be very proud.

Four Single Chants by T. Wardle.

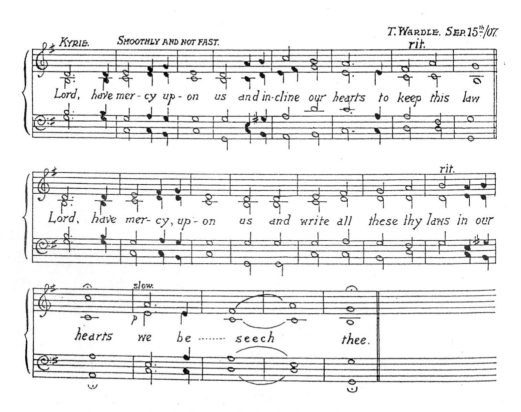

An example of the musical talent of Thomas Wardle

The Straker Steam Bus at Leek Station, 1904.
This bus conveyed passengers to Waterhouses for the Leek and Manifold Light Railway.

The Manifold Valley Railway Train

This photograph shows a section of the narrow guage track at Butterton, with a length of standard guage track for waggons also to be seen. Swainsley is in the background.

A variety of rolling stock of the L&MVLR, at Hulme End

Two Railway Postcard Views of
the Manifold Valley

Swainsley

POSTSCRIPT

Six months after Thomas died, his executors arranged the sale of his major properties on July 7th 1909 at Leek Town Hall. These included 54 St.Edward Street with the adjoining Leek Embroidery Society shop, the empty Hencroft Works, Swainsley and several cottages.

54 St. Edward Street

The sale of the house was complicated by the fact that all three dyeworks had offices there. It was bought by Gilbert, with money lent by his solicitor friend Challinor, for £2,800. The property had enlarged over the years and now consisted of two cottages in the yard and four others, a conservatory, tennis lawn, paddock, stables and a carriage house. For a yearly rent of £25, Gilbert and Horace kept the office accommodation until 1915, when they sold the house to the Maskery brothers from next door (one of whom was a confectioner famous for his gingerbread). After another change of owner when it became a rather sleazy boarding house, it was finally bought by Bowcocks the solicitors, in whose hands it still is. Gilbert moved to Compton House, Cheadle Road, and stayed there till the end of his life.

The shop remained a needlework shop until 1935. After Elizabeth's death in 1902, it was taken over by Mrs Clara Bill, the German lady who had made up the facsimile of the Bayeux Tapestry. She moved the business up the road to No.21 St.Edward Street, and sold it in 1930 to a Mrs Annie Sutton.

Swainsley

All the family loved Swainsley just as Thomas had done. Built in 1867, he had bought the house in 1896 from a Mr.Roscoe. One of the rooms was known as the Rossetti room and there were said to be about fifty pictures attributable to the artist. Most of these were sold in May 1909; two were kept by Gilbert, one was a bequest to the Fitzwilliam Museum in Cambridge, and one was bought by Arthur Lazenby Liberty. The rest are no longer possible to trace, but they had all gone before the house itself was sold two months later.

Margaret Elizabeth Worthington, the Wardle's second daughter and a widow, married Commander Guy Gaunt in 1904 and bought Swainsley after her father's death. They lived there in great style, having added on a ballroom and extended the servants' quarters. One of their nephews wrote that *"Uncle Guy and Aunt Mag came back from the U.S.A. in 1919, and changed its name to Gauntswood. Aunt Mag had great ideas of style. Local farmers' daughters were taken in as I fancy almost unpaid servants. It took two hours to lay the table for dinner. There were several settings. One was naval, with all the gadgets on the table shaped like ships."* He added, *"we were always rather proud of our stately home"*

Brother Fred, who acted as solicitor to all the family, wrote many times over the years urging economy, but the Gaunts went on spending lavishly until finally it had to be sold, probably at the time of the divorce. Lady Gaunt retained the Swainsley cottage and lived there for a while, until she moved back into her old home, now a hotel, as a paying guest. Her bedroom was the previous organ loft added on by her father, the only all-timber room in the house. Tragedy struck; her bed was too near the coal fire. It caught fire and she died in the subsequent blaze. Her charred remains were cremated and her ashes scattered in the Manifold Valley according to her wishes. She was 79 when she died in February 1949, leaving something over £12,000.

Hencroft Works

The Hencroft works in Abbey Green road were very close to the Churnet works of Sir T and A Wardle. Bernard and his brother Tom had worked at the Hencroft for some years, but first Tom then Bernard, left Leek – 'Bernard Wardle and Co.' thrived at New Mills – there is still a firm operating under that name. Hence the Hencroft building lay empty at the time of the sale. Various enterprises were set up there; a tannery, a hose finishing plant and most recently – a cardboard box manufacturer. Nothing now remains of the Hencroft Works.

The Railway

The Leek and Manifold Light Railway never fulfilled the hopes of its investors. The result of Thomas' last intervention in July 1908 when he went to see Lloyd George at the Treasury was not announced, but a few months after his death the following year, the Treasury suspended interest on its loan and the Stoke City Council likewise suspended its interest for five years. This kept the railway going for a while, but a new issue of 4% debenture stock failed to interest many investors. When Colonel Bill, the chairman, died in 1915, the overdraft of £6,508 was paid from his estate since he had guaranteed it personally. The opening of a creamery at Ecton caused a temporary upturn in the fortunes of the little railway, but in 1934 it was forced to close.

Kashmir

The Kashmiri silk industry did well for the next few years after Thomas' death. 1915 was the peak year for production and after that there was a gradual decline (between 1925 and 1935 the price of cocoons fell by almost 50%), despite the fact that the reeling procedure was efficient in Kashmir, as compared to the methods in Bengal described as primitive by the Tariff Commission. It is interesting that Thomas' words were still being quoted in 1935; in particular, his insistence on State control for the industry had proved to be right. New problems had arisen however, and the Silk Manufacturing Company of Srinegar pressed the tariff board in 1935 for a raised duty on foreign imports to combat the Japanese 'dumping' of their silk on the Indian market. They also proposed a discriminatory duty on power loom products in order to protect handloom work. Neither measures were adopted, but the general decline of the silk industry everywhere was inevitable with the advent of man-made fibre.

Lydia

Lydia continued to live in Leek until her death in 1940. In late middle age, she decided, in 1932, that it was lamentable for there to be no public display of Leek embroidery in the town. Nothing remained to show future generations what her mother's work had been like (except of course the church embroideries still in use). She approached Arthur Vinen, then in charge of the Nicholson Institute, but received a cool reply; the piece of the Bayeux Tapestry that she offered would be acceptable, and also a specimen of Lady Wardle's Leek embroidery, as long as they were offered as donations. Obviously, no money was available.

The rebuff made Lydia all the more determined, and within a year she had promoted a retrospective exhibition of Leek embroidery at the Nicholson Institute. Her two surviving sisters, Lady Gaunt and Mrs Horace Wardle, both lived locally and helped her with the task of assembling the exhibits. In June 1933, the Staffordshire Sentinel described the exhibition, full of praise for the forgotten beauty of the old work. The Leek Post came out with big headlines:

THE LEEK EMBROIDERY SOCIETY
2000 YEAR OLD DESIGNS. PICTURES IN SILK.

A quotation from the article is worth recording: *'the success of the school must be traced to the indefatigable labours of Lady Wardle.......It is doing no injustice to her loyal assistants to credit the founder of the school with her due share in the result'.* The words are almost the same as those used by Sir Philip Cunliffe-Owen fifty years previously. The paper's headline of '2000 year old designs' refered to the Ajanta pattern, brought back from Bombay by Thomas in his sketchbook. The example on display had been worked by Mrs Hunt, the lady who had joined the paid embroideresses when in financial straits after she was left a widow. Some of the other exhibits were:

1. A firescreen and table centre stitched by Elizabeth herself and designed by William Morris.
2. The photograph of Elizabeth with her pupils in a tussur embroidered frame.
3. A stole designed by Tom Wardle, Junior, worked by his sister Margaret (Lady Gaunt) for the Rev W.B.Wright, borrowed from All Saints Church, Leek.
4. The Queen Anne design, worked by Miss Annie Redfern.
5. Nine orders of angels, by Miss Winterbottom, late of the Convent in Stone, who had taught at one time in the Embroidery School.
6. A reproduction panel of part of the Bayeux Tapestry, worked by Mrs Billing.

Having resuscitated interest in the past glories of Leek Embroidery, Lydia and her sisters collected a representative selection of the work and presented it to the Nicholson Institute in June 1938 as a small permanent exhibition. With the assistance of her brother Fred, she compiled a description of the Leek School of Embroidery which was framed and hung near the newly presented pieces. This little display is the only example of the work that can be seen publicly. Special exhibitions are arranged from time to time in Leek, either at the Institute or in one of the churches. The main exhibits are the church furnishings, though there are a few smaller domestic items in private ownership. Very little Leek work remains after such a large output, but this is not really surprising considering the transitory nature of domestic items – they either wear out or go out of fashion. But what is really strange is that only three examples of Leek embroidery are owned by the Victoria and Albert Museum. Considering the friendship of Sir Philip Cunlife-Owen with the Wardles, it is puzzling that there was no legacy of Leek work to pass on to the new museum when it supplanted the old South Kensington one where he had been the director for many years.

Sources:

Kashmir: Its new silk industry, natural history, geology, sport, etc.
                        by Thomas Wardle
                        Pub. 1904, London: Simpkin, Marshall, Kent and Co.
                        Leek: WH Eaton, The Moorlands Press, Derby Street.

The North Staffordshire Field Club Records, Salt Library, Stafford.

Parish Records   Cheddleton and Leek, St Edwards.

The Joshua Wardle Papers   Staffs County Record Office.

Lichfield Diocesan Archives

History of Trade Unionism in the North Staffs Textile Industry   F Burchill

Leek Times   Various cuttings

The Leek Embroidery Society   Booklet by Keele University

Nicholson Institute Files Information on Sir Thomas and Lady Wardle and the
                        Bayeux Tapestry

Madeleine Smith   H Blyth

Shrewsbury Local Record Office

Embroidery of the 19th century   Santina Levey

Royal School of Needlework

British Library

Victoria Library, Archives Dept.

Victoria and Albert Museum

Articles from contemporary issues of Studio, Ladies Field, The Lady and The Queen

Exhibition catalogues

India Office   References from files

Indian Tariff Board Enquiry 1932-36

Morris-Wardle correspondence

Life of William Morris   JW Mackail. Pub. Longmans 1911

William Morris Textiles   Linda Parry. Pub. Weidenfield and Nicholson

Wardle Collection of Pattern Books   Whitworth Art Gallery, University of Manchester

Crewel Embroidery in England   Joan Edwards. Pub. Batsford

In Memoriam of Rev. Boucher   Thomas Wardle   Nicholson Institute

On Sewage Treatment and Disposal   Thomas Wardle

Records from the Leek and Manifold Light Railway   Staffs County Record Office

Correspondence re 71 New Bond Street   Between Wardle and Brough, Staffs Record Office

Leek and Manifold Light Railway   Keith Turner   Pub. David and Charles 1980

366 Easy and Inexpensive Dinners: arranged for young homekeepers.   Elizabeth Wardle